Natural Economy

The
Natural Economy

by

JOHN YOUNG

SHEPHEARD-WALWYN

First published in 1997 by
Shepheard-Walwyn (Publishers) Ltd.
26 Charing Cross Road, Suite 34
London WC2H 0DH

British Library Cataloguing-in-Publication Data

A Catalogue record of this book
is available from the British Library

ISBN   0 85683 166 2

Printed and bound in Great Britian by
BPC Wheatons Ltd., Exeter

Contents

Introduction

It is easier to take a watch to pieces than to put it together; and it is easier to see current social problems than to see their solutions. We may even be inclined to doubt that some have solutions.

There are unhappy little children from broken homes, there are people afraid to go out at night because of violent crime, there are lost and lonely individuals driven to suicide by the alienation so common in modern life. In politics, scandal after scandal erupts involving people who are supposed to be leading the nation, while the instances increase of state inference with personal freedom.

In the economic sphere (the subject of this book) we need to be concerned about the public debt, monopolistic practices, taxation, inflation, high interest rates, land prices, recessions, unemployment, poverty. These are not academic problems, but issues affecting everyone, from the young couple struggling to buy a home as land prices and interest rates soar, to the retirees anxiously watching their savings being devoured by inflation.

I maintain that solutions exist and that we can discover what they are. We cannot conduct laboratory experiments, but we can learn from observation and from economic experiments. The collapse of the former Soviet Union was largely the result of the failure of an economic experiment. It had rested on the hypothesis that central planning could do away with the market. It failed in two respects: one, it was less efficient than the Western market-based system; two, it could not in fact suppress markets completely, but spawned black markets which had many undesirable side effects. The significance of that economic experiment and its failure is to demonstrate that no amount of economic theory can change economic fact.

In seeking solutions we are not reduced to finding ideas no one has ever proposed before. It is rather a matter of perceiving which of the already suggested ideas are correct. And one will be helped immensely by treating the subject as a form of "nature study". In other words, we should look at the nature of the basic realities pertaining to economics, and draw conclusions accordingly.

To illustrate. Suppose a doctor disregarded the nature of the human organ being treated, or disregarded the nature of the body as a whole. The diagnosis and treatment would be worse than useless. They might kill the patient. Now suppose well-intentioned people, and some not well-intentioned, persuade the government that subsidies should be given to struggling farmers. Will this bring greater prosperity? Will it cause unwanted surpluses? If surpluses occur, will their donation to poor countries bring even worse hardship there? To answer these questions we need an insight into the nature of the economic realities with which we are dealing, just as the doctor needs an insight into medical realities to provide the right diagnosis and treatment. The investigation has to go beyond economics and look at human society as a whole, at the person and at the meaning of the common good. For economic life does not exist independently of other realities, so it cannot be seen rightly unless it is seen in relation to those other things.

In economics itself, we must analyse the key concepts of competition, price, wealth, capital, money, and so on. The purpose will be to understand the basic truths of economic society, and therefore how a healthy economy can be achieved.

The approach is philosophical. That is, it concentrates on the underlying principles and seeks to determine what ought to be, ethically speaking - not merely what is. The approach is uncommon today, but has a long history. Plato and Aristotle viewed economic questions from this perspective, seeing them intimately related to morality. The great thinkers of the medieval and Renaissance periods did the same. And Adam Smith (1723 - 1790), who has the best claim to the title of father of economic science, was a professor of moral philosophy, and in that capacity delivered the lectures from which his masterpiece *The Wealth of Nations* developed.

Economics has been called the dismal science. It should instead be seen as the study of a marvellous order in human affairs. Economic life is the fundamental part of that great social whole which is human society; and a true grasp of how the economy should be constituted shows it to be a thing of harmony and beauty, all its parts cooperating for the common good, and its inbuilt laws distributing benefits equitably. All the society's other activities - recreational, cultural, political - depend on the economy, somewhat as all the activities of a human being depend on basic nutritional functions. Without satisfactory nutrition the other functions, including those involving the highest exercise of mind and will, become sick and enfeebled. Similarly in society, the further an economy moves from the order proper to it, the greater will be the maladies at every level of the social body.

1

The Principal Agent:
The Free Person

Economic science deals with the production and distribution of goods and services. But this is done by and for human beings. It follows, then, that it is man who is principally to be considered in economics: as working, as investing, as associating with others, and as the end for whom goods and services are intended. Since, however, the study of man goes far beyond economics, the economist has to presuppose certain fundamentals about human nature. It is rather like the discipline of medicine presupposing physiology.

These more basic truths afford an insight into economics, showing us the kind of being who is operating in providing his needs, and thus we see his motivations more clearly, and also get an appreciation of the place of economic activity relatively to human life in general.[1]

A Being of Intellect and Will

We learn what something is by observing what it does. But human beings manifest powers of thinking and willing which show them to transcend the material universe. We have a power of understanding, although imperfectly, the natures of things, and of forming universal concepts. We are not restricted to grasping *this good thing* (this plate of porridge) or *this beautiful thing* (this red rose). The intellect goes beyond the concrete particulars to the universals manifested by them. It grasps, for example, the meaning of goodness or beauty.

Similarly, the will appreciates and is drawn towards goodness without limit; it is not restricted to the (always imperfect) goodness of this or that individual thing we experience. Hence man is the unsatisfied animal: nothing short of infinite goodness would satisfy him, and this is not found in any material thing, or in any collection of material things. Hence he is the progressive animal, striving to improve his condition. I may feel contented with a spring watch that loses ten seconds a day - until I hear about a digital watch that loses ten seconds a year.

Because the intellect sees beyond the individual objects contacted by the senses, understanding that their goodness is imperfect; and because, consequently, the will is not fully satisfied by the objects presented to it, we have freedom of will. That is, the will is not fixed to a particular decision, but is able to choose among objects. No thing, in the way it is known to us, perfectly fulfils our desire for the good, and therefore does not draw us irresistibly. The capacity to choose evil also exists, because a bad thing can be seen as good in some respect. An employer who robs his workers is seeking something he finds good or attractive, such as more wealth for himself or his family.

Yet together with freedom of will (the ability to choose among alternatives), we have a sense of personal responsibility. We know that although we are capable of many choices, not all are fitting exercises of human freedom. Some things violate standards of moral goodness, and therefore ought not to be done. We should act in accordance with what is fitting for human nature; and some actions are not.

Human rights flow from our nature; that is, are due to us because of the kind of being we are. Therefore they are prior to every legal enactment and to the customs of particular communities, as indicated by the fact that we judge certain actions to be wrong even though they be in accordance with the laws or customs of the society in question. Slavery, for instance, is seen as an unjust system regardless of the legal position or the common view in a society that practices it. It is seen as wrong because it violates human rights that exist independently of any legal enactment. Similarly, war criminals are tried because they are judged to have violated human rights, even though they may have acted in full accord with the laws of their country.

So the human person is a being transcending the material universe, a being of intellect and will, a being with inherent rights and responsibilities, a being possessing a dignity that all have an obligation to respect. He is not a mere means to an end, not a "hand" to be used like a machine. He must be allowed the autonomy demanded by his nature. It can never be right for him to be completely subject to any human being or any group.

A Member of a Species

The person transcends society, but is also a bodily being who belongs to a species. In this respect he is part of a whole. Moreover, he is a social animal, adapted to life in a community and unable to fulfil himself independently of the community. As Aristotle says: "He who is unable to live in society, or has no need because he is sufficient for himself, must be either a beast or a god."[2] In the helplessness of the early years, the individual could not exist without others; for the whole of life he needs them to have more than a wretched existence. Other people are needed not only for one's physical well-being, but for one's general development. The mind, the will, the emotions, the total personality: all require interaction with others for their development.

The family. Personal development is achieved through two societies especially, the first of which is the family. Here the individual's earliest and most lasting education takes place - the development of the basic potentialities. Here one is nurtured physically, here one learns to speak and communicate, here the mind is furnished with knowledge, the will learns to love, the emotions are elevated and guided. Through association with the other members of the family and with other relatives, perhaps especially grandparents, the individual receives a share in the living traditions passed down from earlier generations.

The family is a natural society. It is in a different category from, say, a football club. This too is a society or association, but it arises from will, not from nature; there is no drive in human nature towards the establishment of a football club, no frustration of nature if it is not done. It appeals to some people in some situations, but is no more than that. But human nature is structured towards family life. Man and woman are complementary to each other, not just physically, but emotionally and intellectually. That is why they are attracted to each other in all those ways. Moreover, this natural attraction tends to a permanent union: a man and woman who are in love want that state to last. Further, it is an exclusive union: a union of one man and one woman. And it is biologically ordered to the generation of children.

It follows that the parents are by nature the primary educators. Love for their children, with the desire to give them the very best, makes them uniquely suited to provide for their education. The home, indeed, is the best milieu for education, because of the close relationship between the members of the family. Actually, it is not just a matter of the parents educating the children, but of each member contributing to the education of all the others - by what they are rather than by direct instruction.

Scepticism is often expressed today about the value of the family, although more often by academics than by people in general. Admittedly no family is ideal; but this indicates the need to strengthen family life. When the law allows easy divorce, or economic conditions make it necessary for mothers to join the work force, great damage is done to the family, and therefore to society. George Gilder contends that "upward mobility depends on three principles - work, family, and faith...These are the pillars of a free economy and a prosperous society."[3]

Civil society. The family is one natural society, but there is another: civil society, or the state. This too is demanded by human nature for its fulfilment, because individuals and families alone are not adequate for the purpose. Laws are needed to guide social life, police and military forces are needed for protection, large community organisations are required for the development of the potential of the people. Looking at the individual, we find four levels or strata, and to each of these corresponds a level or stratum of civil society.

The individual has *vegetative life*, like the plants, and the basic element here is nutrition. He has *sensitive life*, like the lower animals, with powers of sight and the other external senses, together with imagination, memory and emotional powers. Superior to these capabilities he has *intellect and will*, as we noted earlier. The intellect may be turned to pursuits that *do not issue directly in any action or product* - for example, the acquisition of knowledge for its own sake, or to other cultural ends. Or it may be employed for the *practical purposes of doing or making*. Now, looking at human society, we find important correspondences.

The economic order is analogous to the nutritive life of the individual. Consider the most necessary function of the economy, the provision of food. We have higher needs than this, but without nourishment we wouldn't be alive to exercise them. Another way in which the economic order is like the nutritive functions of the individual is in the support given to higher things. Just as the individual is able to exercise higher functions through the strength given by food, so the economic order provides the means for cultural and other activities, as when books are produced for education, or economic efficiency allows leisure for activities we would not otherwise have had time for.

The second level or stratum of civil society is what we can call the recreational, embracing all those social activities that come under the heading of recreation. This has a correspondence to the sensitive life of the individual, because recreation is primarily about the refreshment and renewal of the sensible faculties, especially imagination and the emotional powers. The refreshment of these aids the other powers. So when sports and other forms of recreation arise in society, this is a social help to the renewal of the members of the community.

The third level can broadly be called the cultural, and corresponds to the employment of the mind in "non-productive" ways. It comprises those social activities which aim directly to perfect the highest human powers - those of intellect and will - and include art, fine literature, music, philosophy, religion.

The fourth level is the political: the governing functions of the community - local, state, federal (and to some degree international) - and including the system of laws. This is analogous to the intellect of the individual used for practical purposes. Just as the individual makes practical judgments about what to do, the governing bodies of civil society have the task of judging about the activities of the community. It is a very honourable task, surprising as that statement may seem when one sees what politics is like in practice. The trouble is that there is no agreement as to what are the tasks of the politicians, and consequently they usurp the place of others, especially in economic matters; which leads to all manner of corruption. But the true tasks of politics, concerned as they are with the promotion of justice and peace in the community, are tasks of great value.

Viewing civil society as a whole, with its four levels, it appears as a fascinating organism, bestowing wonderful benefits on its members, benefits usually taken for granted, but whose importance can be better appreciated if we imagine ourselves without them. If we subtract, in our thought, all the economic, recreational, cultural and political benefits we enjoy, and think of the meagre results from struggling through life in isolation from society, the treasures we now enjoy shine more clearly. A solitary adult would be fortunate to survive at all, and it would be a wretched existence. A family would be immeasurably better off than one person, especially in non-economic social benefits, but it would be a life of deprivation, culturally and otherwise. And in so far as cultural benefits were enjoyed, this would be due largely to the fact that they had passed down from previous generations. Take away that heritage and even the family would scarcely be above the level of brute animals.

A sense of patriotism should be the response to the benefits our country gives us. Our country deserves our love, our appreciation, our service. I don't like flag burning, not even the flag of a country with a totalitarian regime, for the flag represents far more than the political regime. It represents the nation, with all its values and goodness. Much will be wrong with it (much is wrong with every nation); but the evils, vast though they may be, will not outweigh the good. If we suspect otherwise, we should reflect again on life without the benefits our country has brought us.

When Horace said, "It is sweet and right to die for one's country",[4] he was expressing a sentiment deeply rooted in human nature. The act of dying for one's country, when the cause is just, is a noble act.

The Person and Society

There may seem a contradiction between what has been said about the importance of the community and what was said earlier about the free person. It seems that the person is not so free after all: he is dependent on the family and the state, is subject to authority, and in a war may be acting well by sacrificing his life for the nation. Now to solve this apparent discrepancy, we need to examine more closely the relationship between the human being as a person and as a part of society.

Consider a nest of ants or a colony of bees. Each ant or bee is part of a whole, and is for the sake of the whole. If a bee can no longer function in the service of the hive, it will be thrown out to die. Now, coming to human society, we see that the individual, like the ant or the bee, is part of the whole, and is ordered towards the good of the whole. The very notion of a part is of something for the sake of the whole: part has no meaning except in relation to whole. Precisely as a member of a species, therefore, each of us is for the sake of the species, as in the rest of nature; and precisely as a member of civil society each of us is for the sake of society. So society has a moral right to make laws that bind its members, and a right to take punitive action against them if they disobey. These powers are necessary to safeguard the good of the whole.

Yet the human person transcends the material universe, for he is a being of intellect and will. So he cannot be totally subject to society. An image may arise of society as a giant reality to which all its members are subservient; but of course it is not like that at all. Society is an association of persons, with no existence apart from them. In serving society we are serving persons; and society itself, at all levels, is for the sake of persons. So government is for the governed, not for the governors; and the economy is for all its participants, not for privileged groups.

Individualism stresses the autonomy of the unit, the individual or person, and fights against oppression by government authorities. Unfortunately, it views human society as the sum total of the individuals comprising it, rather than as a social organism united by the pursuit of a common good.

The interdependence of the members is not adequately seen, nor is the subordination of the part (the individual) to the whole. Ayn Rand exemplifies this viewpoint,[5] with her constant emphasis on the autonomy of the individual and the "virtue of selfishness".

Collectivism, on the other hand, puts the emphasis on society as a whole, and the subordination of the individual. Benito Mussolini, therefore, was able to say, in his *La dottrina del Fascismo*, that the state is "the true reality of the individual", and the Fascist state is "the highest and most potent form of personality." Furthermore, "Nothing human or spiritual, in so far as it has any value, exists outside the state."[6] Collectivism is a bee hive concept, leaving little initiative for the persons who compose society, as we see in its best example, Marxism.

Michael Novak emphasises both the communitarian and the personal. "The very purpose of a true community is to nourish in its midst the full development of each person among its members. Conversely, it is in the nature of the human person - an originating source of knowing and loving - to be in communion with others, who share in his or her knowing and loving."[7]

References

[1] The importance of a holistic view of human nature for the economist is examined in *Social Economics: Retrospect and Prospect*, edited by Mark A. Lutz, Boston, Kluwer Academic Publishers, 1990.

[2] Aristotle, *Politics*, book I, chapter 2, 1253a, 29.

[3] George Gilder,*Wealth and Poverty*, New York, Basic Books, 1981, p. 74.

[4] Horace, *Odes,* book III, ode 2, verse 13.

[5] She expresses her outlook vividly in *The Fountainhead* and her other novels, and more directly in her non-fiction, such as *The Virtue of Selfishness*.

[6] Quoted by Jacques Maritain, *Integral Humanism*, Indiana, University of Notre Dame Press, 1973, p. 135.

[7] Michael Novak, *This Hemisphere of Liberty*, Washington DC, American Enterprise Institute for Public Policy Research, 1990, p. 18.

2

The Common Good

When the term *common good* is used, it is generally left unexplained, as though its meaning were evident to everyone. Actually, I am sure that even the person who employs the term is in most cases vague as to what is meant.

The same word can be used in various senses, and I am not claiming that common good has to be understood in the precise sense in which I intend to employ it. But the reality I want to discuss has to be understood if society, including the economy, is to be understood; and common good is an excellent name for that reality. It has a relation to the expression *public good* as used by economists, which is a commodity or a service available to everyone, even non-payers; and one person's consumption does not lessen that of others.[1]

Johannes Messner uses the term in a sense rather similar to mine, and sees the concept as central to an understanding of society. The importance he attaches to it is evident from the fact that in the index to his *Social Ethics* the entries under *common good* occupy three quarters of a page.[2]

Meaning of the Common Good
It can be defined: **A non-exclusive benefit, desired as a social end, and achieved through association.**

Suppose we are considering a voluntary society (as distinct from a natural one); say a Shakespearian group. Its common good could be expressed as: "Appreciation of the works of Shakespeare." This conforms to the definition, as we see on analysis of the three elements contained there.

A non-exclusive benefit. No matter how much one member gains in the appreciation of Shakespeare, this does not limit the appreciation the other members can have. Rather, it enhances it, because the person who gains a lot will tend to spread what is gained. It is unlike a material commodity, such as a table or chair, where one person's possession excludes or restricts that of others. This non-appropriative, or non-restrictive, feature of the common good is its fundamental characteristic, which must be grasped if one is to understand the term common good as used here. Reflect on friendship or patriotism or peace or knowledge. In each case the same quality is present: the quality of being capable of possession by any number of people without diminution of what each receives.

If I want to share knowledge with nine other people, I need have no fear that I will lose it by doing so. We can all have it. It is not like sharing money with them. Ten pounds shared with nine people will result in ninety per cent of it being lost to me; whereas knowledge shared with them will remain mine while becoming theirs. If in practice everyone does not receive equally, it won't be due to the nature of the good, but to other causes, such as differing degrees of ability.

Desired as a social end. This is the second element in our definition. The common good is desired in common by the members of the group; that is, it constitutes the end or object, the *raison d'être*, of the group. A genuine member of the Shakespearian society desires an "appreciation of the works of Shakespeare". Should the point be reached where a large percentage of the members do not want this, but are there for other reasons, the group is likely to change into something else.

Achieved through association. The members do not attain it as individuals, but as associated with one another; as a society: they achieve it in common. Each contributes talents, encouragement, and so on, and all the contributions are "socialised" into a whole which is more than a collection of individual bits. Particularly when a group is really keen, it generates a spirit which is of great help in gaining the desired end. Anyone who thinks that the "appreciation of the works of Shakespeare" which results from the group's efforts is just the effect of the sum total of individual efforts is badly astray. Association has within itself a dynamism deriving from the individuals, yet transcending them.

So the common good is common in three ways: It is common in its nature (distributively as opposed to collectively - is of such a nature that its possession by one does not limit its possession by others); it is common as an end desired (this common end is what makes something be a society and not merely a gathering of individuals); and it is achieved or actualised in common (not by a collection of individual efforts).

Briefly, and now putting the elements in order of attainment, it is commonly desired; commonly achieved; commonly possessed. It can be defined alternatively as **a good desired in common, achieved in common, and possessed in common**.

Private Property and Public Property. Before coming to the economic common good, we will contrast private and public property with the common good. We need to define four terms: ownership, property, public property, private property.

Ownership: **The right to possess, use and dispose of a thing**. So if a person rents something - a house, for instance - his right to possess and use it is subject to conditions. And he has no right to dispose of it. Absolute ownership, on the contrary, would carry with it complete freedom in all three respects. In fact limitations are imposed on owners, for other people have rights too; but provided the limitations are not very severe it would be unreasonable to say that ownership had been nullified.

Property, the second of the terms under discussion, can be defined: **things over which is had the right of possession, use and disposal**. These may be owned either publicly or privately, so we must distinguish the two.

Public property is: **Property owned by a society**. We think especially of things owned by the state: roads, government buildings, public parks, and so on; but the definition applies also to the property of any other society, including business companies. For the essential point is that a society - that is, an organised group, united by an end - is the owner of the property, because it is the group as such, not the individuals who comprise it, that has the right to possess, use and dispose of the property. If I own shares in a company, I have a right to those shares, but no right to walk into the factory and start operating the machinery. Or if I decide to migrate, I cannot demand a share of the public goods of the country I am leaving.

Private property is: **Property owned by one or more individuals, not by a society**. Or: **Property owned individually**. There may be joint owners, but the essential thing is that a society does not have the right of possession, use and disposal.

Comparing the two, public property is directed to the common good of the society: this is its primary orientation or purpose; whereas private property is directed primarily to the good of individuals. The roads, the government buildings and so on are not for the sake of particular groups, but are meant to serve the common good, a position which is violated when the people's money is lavished on ostentatious projects for the purpose of glorifying the nation's leaders. Professor Bauer says of Third World debt defaulters: "The countries of the defaulters are littered with monuments and relics of unviable and grandiose schemes undertaken for the political and personal purposes of the rulers and their local allies, often promoted by western commercial interests. This is such a well-worn and well-documented theme that details would be otiose."[3] As for private property, it too should serve the common good, but this effect, although of vital importance, is indirect. If I own a business, it will firstly be for my benefit, and will also serve the common good. More basically, the satisfaction, incentive and security given the individual by ownership contribute to the welfare of the whole society.

Is there such a thing as common property? No; not in the sense in which the word common is used here. For property means something appropriated, something from which non-owners are to a greater or lesser extent excluded. But the common, from its nature, excludes none. Inequality of participation is never from the nature of the common good. If one member of the Shakespearian company shares less than another in the good it generates, this will be due to such factors as taking less interest, having less ability, being unable to attend as regularly, being cold-shouldered by other members.

Economic Common Good

Having viewed the common good in general, we come now to the economy. Is there a common good which gives direction to the economic system? Is there more than one such good?

Well, what is the economy all about? It is for the production of goods and services. Why do people cooperate to produce them, rather than each person working alone? Because the isolated individual (assuming he could survive) would work with greater difficulty, for longer hours, and without being able to produce many things made possible by cooperation with others. Society results in an *abundance of goods and services*, with the gaining of *leisure*, and with a *saving of effort* in production. Let us look separately at these, relating them to the common good.

Abundance of goods and services (or wealth and services). This is a common good, for it is commonly desired, commonly achieved, and commonly possessed.

Firstly, it is commonly desired (that is, desired as a social end). Just as the end of the Shakespearian group is "appreciation of Shakespeare's works", the aim of economic society is to have an abundance of goods and services. The individual, with rare exceptions, will desire a moderate abundance for himself, and will usually desire that the whole society be well supplied. Certainly he should do so, and society will suffer to the extent that individuals ignore the advancement of all. Further, there is a deeper sense in which this abundance is the end of economic society: the economy tends to it from its nature. A rightly constituted economy, as our next consideration will bring out, is intrinsically ordered to an abundance of goods and services.

Secondly, the abundance is commonly achieved (achieved as a social end). Many people working together can do what is beyond the power of the same number working separately. Also, differing interests and talents can be utilised when many people combine, whereas in separation each will be unable to do numerous important things through lack of ability, while lacking the opportunity to exercise skills he does have. Specialisation becomes highly developed in society, with the person who, in isolation, would have been a jack of all trades and master of none becoming an expert in a chosen field. And natural advantages of climate, soil and so on can be harnessed through trade with distant places. Likewise, economies of scale make vast savings possible.

Thirdly, the abundance resulting from cooperation constitutes a benefit which is commonly possessed (a non-exclusive benefit). From its nature it is open to all in the community. Think of the ease with which we can obtain our wants through the social economy; think of the variety of products and services available.

Leisure. The economy gives us leisure. This, too, is a common good.

It is commonly desired (desired as a social end). The individual desires it for himself - even the workaholic wants some leisure; and if not very selfish we will desire it for other people. More fundamentally, the social organism which is the economy tends to the creation of leisure. Economic efficiency results in time over after earning a living. This benefit flows from the nature of the economy.

Leisure is also commonly achieved (achieved as a social end). The social factors that produce an abundance of goods and services are at the same time productive of leisure. A few hours' work per day give a result that would be unattainable even if one could labour twenty-four a day in a solitary state.

The third characteristic of a common good - its quality of being commonly possessed, a non-exclusive benefit - is found in the leisure made possible by the economy. Of itself it is available for all; only extrinsic causes, including injustice, block some from fully sharing in this bounty.

Leisure does not mean laziness. The economist cannot tell us how we should employ our freedom from economic activity, but a larger perspective shows the essential place of leisure in the development of the best human qualities. From that larger perspective Josef Pieper says: "Leisure, it must be remembered, is not a Sunday afternoon idyll, but the presence of freedom, of education and culture, and of that undiminished humanity which views the world as a whole."[4] George Soule, writing of the time saved by technology from earning a living, claims: "This is indeed a revolution. Conceivably it can lead to disaster." But if the time is well used, a civilization may be produced, "The like of which has never been seen, and which dreamers have scarcely been able to imagine."[5]

Saving of effort. Before examining this in the economy we need to view the saving of effort in a wider sense, for it applies in all areas of life.

Effort as such is unpleasant, for it means struggle, arduousness, difficulty. Effort cannot be wanted for its own sake, as there is no attractiveness in it. Certainly it can present an attractive challenge, as in climbing Mount Everest or swimming the English Channel, but the desired object is the triumph over difficulties through strength and skill. Whenever we see that our aim can be attained either by an easy means or with difficulty, we choose the easy means. At first glance this may seem dubious, but reflection shows it to be true.

Suppose I walk the long way home instead of taking the short cut. Am I choosing effort for its own sake? No; there is always another factor. Perhaps I want exercise, or to admire the scenery, or to fill in time; perhaps I enjoy walking.

The crucial point is this: effort as such is necessarily seen as unattractive, and therefore as unable to be chosen. For only that which is perceived, rightly or wrongly, to have some attractive quality can be chosen as an end. Only the attractive attracts. Whenever effort is chosen, it is as a means to an end.

The principle of the saving of effort is a key to economic behaviour. Each person wants to save effort. The worker seeks a job which, on balance, will be less arduous than others available. The investor seeks the best return, so as to have greater means of satisfying desires more easily. The business owner wants more efficient capital equipment so that effort will be saved.

The principle must be seen in a total context. When we say the worker opts for the least arduous job, account is being taken of a complex of factors. He will consider the hours worked, the money earned, travelling distances, whether shift work is involved. The pleasantness or unpleasantness of the working environment will be assessed. Satisfactions will be balanced against dissatisfactions. Even the effort anticipated in searching for a better job will influence the decision about seeking a change of employment. Similarly, some people do not put their funds in the objectively most desirable investment because they cannot be bothered doing the necessary research and transferring of funds.

Although we know a certain course of action can be expected to save effort in the long term, we may opt for a short term saving of effort, as this tends to draw us more powerfully. The principle under discussion does not mean we always act in the most rational way in saving effort.

As a principle of economics it can be defined: **In the economy all participants naturally tend to save effort through exchange**. The economy consists of a network of exchanges, directed to abundance and leisure; and people strive to achieve this with a minimum of effort as they work, invest, buy and sell. The striving is natural, for it is a matter of avoiding something - effort, arduousness, difficulty - which, in itself, can only be seen as totally unattractive. It is natural also because it results in a richer abundance of wealth and services and in more leisure: aims which we seek as common goods.

The saving of effort through exchange has the three characteristics belonging to a common good. It is commonly desired. It is commonly achieved, through the working of the social economy. It is commonly possessed (is a non-exclusive benefit), for its nature is such that it is open to all; a bonus arising from the economy's operation.

Relationship of the three benefits. Three things have been classified as economic common goods. But unless they stand in some relation to each other, how can the economy be unified?

The central one is abundance of goods and services. Subtract this and we would not need an economic system. This is the specific end of the economy. Leisure, however, is an end beyond the economy, for it is **freedom from economic activity**. Saving of effort, by contrast with the other two, is primarily a means, not an end. Although in one respect it is an end (that is, something sought for itself), because freedom from effort is pleasant, its main thrust in economic activity is towards goods and services and towards leisure. It is a means to their attainment.

In every single economic act the desire to save effort is present, at least subconsciously, for reason and instinct alike urge us to achieve results with the minimum of trouble. It is a dynamic principle promoting efficiency throughout the economy, a means to abundance. And in doing this it is a means to that end beyond the economy: namely leisure, or freedom from economic activity.

Attacking the common good. Paradoxically, the desire for these three great benefits can be perverted into attacks on them. This is a constant fact in actual economic life. Wanting these for themselves, people find ways of getting them at the expense of others. Effort can often be saved by imposing it on our fellow participants in the economy, a device which finds its ultimate expression in slavery. We thereby acquire wealth and leisure by taking them from others.

If people are excluded from access to land except on terms the owners choose to set, they are to that extent blocked from sharing in the common good generated by the community. Instead, the owners get the benefit. As access to land is the absolutely basic condition for any participation in the common good, the question of land rights must be settled satisfactorily if the common good is not to be perverted into the enrichment of some at the expense of others.

That perversion can be effected in many ways; for instance, through pressure for excessive wages, through tariff agreements, through restriction of the entry of individuals or firms into areas they should be free to enter.

An understanding of the common good throws a flood of light on the nature of society, its unity, and deviations from the character it ought to have. It also shows the goodness of society, and that the evils with which it is riddled are due to the perversion of the common good, which should flourish so much more than it does. Economists talk a lot about scarcity; but the concentration should be on the benefits, the bounty, society produces, and on how to let this bounty increase by removing the evils that hinder it.

References
1   See, e.g., Donald Rutherford, *Dictionary of Economics*, London, Routledge, 1992.
2   Johannes Messner, *Social Ethics*, London, Herder, 1965.
3   Peter Bauer, *The Third World Debt Crisis*, St Leonards, New South Wales, the Centre for Independent Studies, 1990, p. 5.
4   Josef Pieper, *Leisure the Basis of Culture*, London, Faber and Faber, 1952, p. 59.
5   George Soule, *What Automation Does to Human Beings*, London, Sidgwick and Jackson, 1956, p. 113.

3

Economic Freedom

In chapter one we saw that man, as a being with intellect and will, is entitled to a large measure of autonomy. We need to look now at this right to freedom in regard to making economic decisions. The person, whether as worker, investor or consumer, should be afforded the widest choice consistent with the common good. Otherwise the aspirations for freedom springing from the depths of human nature are frustrated, and social progress is thereby impeded. First let us note various helps to economic liberty and the limitations to liberty that result from their absence, beginning with the fundamental question of private ownership.

Aids to Freedom

Private property encourages initiative and responsibility, qualities which promote freedom in society. Since property involves a right of disposal, those who use property they do not own are more restricted than owners, and therefore less able to exercise initiative. Private ownership also tends to the better utilisation of property for the good of all, because of the keener interest people take in what belongs to them. They will usually take less care of public property and devote less effort to increasing it. A further advantage is that private ownership is a safeguard against oppression. If the state were to own all the means of production it would be the only employer, and if it owned all the real estate it would be the only landlord. In these extreme circumstances it could impose its will on the individual, through the threat of unemployment or eviction. The greater the spread of property, the less potent the state threat to liberty.

It follows that freedom will tend to be strengthened to the extent that individuals have property and weakened to the extent that they lack it. Power tends to be with the property owners. This applies both in relation to public versus private property, and in relation to large private holdings compared with small. Regarding public ownership, while the big danger to freedom is the state, the term public ownership, in the sense discussed earlier, applies also to corporate ownership. Public property was defined: **Property owned by a society**; a concept embracing all cases of group ownership. Hence domination over others is found in big corporations. Both in their case and in that of the state, those who run the group participate in the power of ownership, for ownership, as we saw, is **the right to possess, use and dispose of a thing**. Therefore, to the extent that those ruling a state or running a company have the power of possession, use and disposal, to that extent they have, in practice, a share in ownership, with the domination this affords.

Helmut Leipold, writing of eastern Europe under Communism, discusses the lack of incentives, the political interests, the bureaucratic interference and other defects. He concludes: "The failure of both centrally planned as well as of socialist market systems demonstrates the economic importance and impact of property rights. The transformation of all socialist economies into a workable market economy demands a transformation of ownership rights."[1]

Concerning land ownership, the experience of Third World countries shows starkly the domination owners can exercise over non-owners. In extreme conditions tenants can be forced to pay so much to the owner that they live at or near subsistence level. In these conditions, improvements in production may be no help. Suppose a farmer, by the use of fertiliser, better machinery or more extensive irrigation, gets a thirty per cent increase in his return. The land owner, seeing this, may say: "Now that my land is producing more, I must ask for more rent. It will leave you no worse off, because it will come from the improved production."

R.E. Downs and S.P. Reyna suggest a turning point has been reached for sub-Saharan Africa in the relationship of the people to the land. Land is no longer free; access is becoming more restricted; some are acquiring large amounts while others are losing what they had. "... more and more people are forced to abandon or sell their land to seek their subsistence elsewhere or work as hired laborers on the land of others."[2]

In developed countries too, land ownership confers great power, a fact to be examined later. The producer who owns his land has an advantage over the producer who rents, and the big owner has an advantage over the small; while the owner of his own house and land has more freedom than the person who rents.

The possession of assets is a means to economic freedom, providing a wider range of options: perhaps a business venture, or even simply giving one time to search for a better job. Freedom is drastically restricted if one is forced to live from hand to mouth.

Education is another aid to economic liberty, and its lack restricts liberty, whether it is a matter of general education or of special skills. True education, widely taken, operates to develop the whole personality, including the inculcation of honesty, self-control, initiative. The influence of the social environment and especially of the family is crucial; and a striking difference often appears between individuals of good and bad backgrounds in their handling of economic opportunities. The same difference is seen between ethnic groups, some being far more progressive than others because of factors in their social background.

A survey published in 1989 by A.B. Atkinson compared people whose fathers had been studied twenty-five years earlier, in relation to pay levels. It found, George and Howards report, that "The proportion of children who are low-paid is 50 per cent for those whose fathers are low-paid, compared with 27 per cent for those not low-paid."[3]

Access to work opportunities is a condition of economic freedom, yet access is often blocked unreasonably. Take the shocking injustice of people being forbidden by law to begin learning a trade after a certain age - even as low as seventeen. Of course these impediments are there for a reason: they serve sectional interests, as in keeping wages high by restricting the number of workers to below the market level. The same object is served by the imposition of quotas for those wishing to enter certain professions. Then there are unrealistically high minimum wage laws, making it difficult or impossible for some to gain employment; for employers will not take on a worker they judge to be incapable of earning the wage payable: to do so would be to subsidise the worker.

A *well-functioning economy* is a further help to freedom, whereas disruption reduces freedom. It becomes more difficult to plan ahead, with a greater danger of failing in business or losing one's job. Problems of taxation, high interest rates, inflation, are all enemies of freedom, and the ever-recurring recessions erode it further.

Unhampered trade between nations is of immense assistance to freedom. It provides markets, it allows us to purchase things that might otherwise have been unavailable, it reduces the danger of dominance by a few big firms. Producers in a given country may be able to agree tacitly on measures that will work to their unfair advantage, but it is a great deal harder to devise a workable scheme when products from anywhere in the world are permitted to compete with national industry. The free trade question will be analysed more fully in the following chapter, where objections will be examined to the matters being discussed here.

The Great Obstacle to Freedom

A pervasive obstacle to freedom underlies much of what we have listed, and we can give it the name *privilege*. I would define it as: **A power accorded by the state to some, with undue discrimination against others**.

An instance is that of sectional interests gaining at the expense of other people when access to work opportunities is blocked by legislation - as mentioned above. Again, government restrictions on free trade involve advantages to some with undue discrimination against others.

As well as being directly hampered by privilege, freedom is hampered indirectly. Take the diminishing of freedom through poverty, through poor education, through recessions and other disruptions of the economy. Only too often these are caused by advantages accorded, presently or in the past, by the state to some at the expense of others.

When we speak of a power "accorded by the state", this includes the tacit acceptance by the state of discriminatory measures. If a trade union, for instance, breaks the law to get what it wants, with undue discrimination against others, and the government refuses to intervene, *de facto* power is being given to that union by the state. Further, the government itself may be in a privileged position, for it may give itself powers involving undue discrimination against people.

As we proceed it will become clearer that privilege, as above defined, is the principal cause of economic and political maladies, and that the fight for health in those spheres must be largely a fight for the abolition of privilege.

Competition: True and Spurious

To the extent that economic freedom exists, competition arises; but we need to be clear about the use of the word competition, as it is one of the numerous words employed with a variety of meanings in economics. Economists speak of perfect competition, imperfect competition, monopolistic competition, cutthroat competition, destructive competition. Let us begin by defining the word as used here. **Economic agents, all with a diversity of opportunities open to them, striving through exchange to provide or obtain labour, wealth or services**.

Economic agents: all those involved in the economy, whether workers, investors, consumers. *Striving through exchange*: a distinguishing mark of economic activity is that it involves exchanges, as distinct from the direct satisfaction of one's own needs. *Labour, wealth or services*: these are the subject matter of competition.

The key factor in the definition is expressed in the words *all with a diversity of opportunities*. This diversity is present to the extent that the freedom exists which we have analysed. Unless private property, good education and the other aids to freedom are available, freedom and opportunities will be restricted, and therefore true competition will not flourish. Competition is a property of freedom: a consequence which necessarily flows from freedom, like heat from fire.

In the economy millions of people act for the ends noted earlier: they want an abundance of goods and services, with leisure from economic activities; and they try to save effort in the accomplishment of their wants. Now, suppose each person has a variety of opportunities - whether for work, for investment, for buying goods. Each will utilise those opportunities in obtaining what is desired. Generally speaking, the worker will choose a job that affords better pay and conditions than others are offering, the investor will seek the most satisfactory investment, the buyer will want the best bargain.

Even with each worker and investor seeking to benefit himself, the common good will still be served, because each will benefit himself most by serving others. By using his talents in the optimum way he will give more to society and will therefore be better rewarded by society, through the market. Each person will also be more motivated because he has liberty, in contrast with the lack of incentive found in a slave society, in a socialist economy - or in a capitalist economy with high levels of unemployment.

Spurious competition. There is another reality, opposite to what we have been considering, which can be called spurious competition. Its definition: **Economic agents, lacking diversity of opportunities, striving against each other to provide or obtain labour, wealth or services**. Let us compare the two, which we find mingled together in actual economic life.

Lacking diversity of opportunities. This is the distinctive difference between true and spurious competition. The other differences flow from this. To the extent that I lack opportunities my freedom is narrowed. In an extreme case, if I need work to survive, and only one job is open to me, I have no economic freedom. I either take that job or starve.

Given due diversity, there is genuine market activity: that is, free exchanges are made, and the participants benefit through the process. But when opportunities are lacking, true market activity is restricted, and some are enabled to gain by imposing losses on others. They do not benefit through exchange, but through the restriction of exchange. An association may extort higher pay than the market would give its members; or a firm may so restrict the market that it can get excessively high returns. Some people certainly benefit, but not through the competitive exchange mechanism of the market. They take advantage of the lack of liberty by imposing burdens on others.

Striving against each other. In a sense those engaged in true competition are striving against each other. The point is, though, that this is without the element of struggling for justice, even for survival, found in its spurious imitator. Think of the depression years of the 1930s, or the grim conditions in the first half of the nineteenth century, or the conditions prevailing in many countries today, with a fierce struggle to gain employment.

When people speak of competition as bad, or say it should be controlled, they have this one-sided, so-called competition in mind. Yet it is not really competitive, precisely because it is one-sided. It is bad not because people compete, but because they cannot compete. Suppose I were to praise some mythical country for its competition, and you, wanting to know about it, asked me for details of the social structure. If I were to reply, "Well, for a start, the workers there are all slaves", you would assume, surely, that I was joking. If it were a nation where competition reigned, wouldn't this imply free workers? But suppose I were to say: "The great period of competition and free enterprise was the nineteenth century." My statement might not cause surprise. One thinks of the rugged individualists who made vast fortunes in those days, of the opportunities for initiative, of the alleged flowering of *laissez faire* capitalism.

Ayn Rand claims that "during the nineteenth century, the world came close to economic freedom, for the first and only time in history."[4]

But in reality is there not a close resemblance between the mythical slave economy of my illustration and the real society of nineteenth century industrialism? The average worker had little freedom, especially in the earlier part of the century. He was not entitled to vote, which allowed those with interests opposed to his to dominate in political decision-making; there were laws against the operation of trade unions; he often lacked education; poverty prevented him from holding out for better conditions, as he had to continue working to live, while employers could afford to forgo profits temporarily in the event of a strike. Yet this is seen as the great era of competition and free enterprise!

The Tolpuddle Martyrs didn't think so. They were six English labourers in Dorsetshire who were sentenced in 1834 to seven years' transportation (the sentences were remitted two years later) to an Australian penal colony because they organised trade union activities to protect their meagre wages.[5]

Two opposite realities. Spurious competition is the antithesis of true competition. The true is based on freedom, with a variety of opportunities; the spurious is based on constraint, with a lack of opportunities. The true is effort-saving activity through exchange; the spurious is effort-imposing activity through domination. The true causes equitable distribution and optimal efficiency; the spurious causes inequitable distribution with impaired efficiency.

True competition promotes the common good: the whole society shares in the ease and prosperity that arise. Spurious competition promotes the good of some individuals at the expense of the common good: their power allows them to appropriate what others should get.

The Principle of Subsidiarity

There is a principle which follows from what we have said in this and the previous chapters, and which provides a means of measuring the degree of freedom in society. It is called the principle of subsidiarity, and is formulated: **What can be done by an individual or smaller group should not be assigned to a larger group**.

It applies both in economics and beyond. It means, for instance, that families must be allowed to manage their own affairs without intervention by the state unless justice requires intervention. It means that if private enterprise can do a task, it should not be done by the government; and if local or state authorities can handle it, the federal government should leave it to them. It also opposes concentration of power in a few big firms. Larger groups, and particularly the government, should be subsidiary to smaller groups - should assist and supplement them where needed, but only where needed. "The principle of subsidiarity…is a concept that all social economists may want to take to heart and mind," says Mark Lutz.[6]

The foundation of the principle is the nature of the human person: a being with intelligence and free will, and who, because of these powers, is entitled to autonomy. Of course there are limits, but liberty should not be restricted without necessity - as though the government knew better than we do how our lives should be run. People differ in their aptitudes, interests, needs and opportunities, and know their own situation better than some controlling body could know it. They act, too, with more drive and initiative when unhampered. Left to make their own decisions, they usually develop a greater sense of responsibility. Given these truths about the human person, the principle of subsidiarity follows logically.

References

[1] Helmut Leipold, "Some institutional failures of socialist market economies..." in *Reform and Transformation in Eastern Europe*, edited by Kovacs and Tardos, London, Routledge, 1992, p. 89.

[2] *Land and Society in Contemporary Africa*, edited by Downs and Reyna, Hanover, University of New Hampshire, 1988, p. 16.

[3] V. George and I. Howards, *Poverty Amidst Affluence*, Aldershot, Edward Elgar, 1991, p. 33.

[4] Ayn Rand, *For the New Intellectual*, New York, Signet Books, 1963, p. 25.

[5] See *The New Encyclopaedia Britannica*, 1994, under **Tolpuddle Martyrs.**

[6] *Social Economics: Retrospect and Prospect*, edited by Mark A. Lutz, Boston, Kluwer Academic Publishers, 1990, p. 431.

4

Objections to Competition

Objections are often voiced against the contention that competition should be allowed full scope; and the discussion is frequently made more difficult by the fact that the protagonists have conflicting concepts of competition. Emotional overtones further complicate the issue.

Most people would feel repulsion against the nineteenth century doctrine of the so-called iron law of wages. David Ricardo (1772 - 1823) explains that when wages are high the working population will increase, for there will be a lower death rate; but then the increased population, competing for the available work, will force wages down, until the resulting privations increase the death rate and thereby reduce the number of workers. A further wage rise follows. Ricardo thought it impossible to change this law, and stated that, like all contracts, "wages should be left to the fair and free competition of the market, and should never be controlled by the interference of legislature."[1]

Note the words "fair and free competition". The labourers were struggling for survival, yet the conditions were supposed to be fair and free! As for competition, this was the spurious competition analysed in the previous chapter, the antithesis of the genuine competition whose hallmark is freedom of choice.

Many other moral teachers would concur with the judgment of Pope Pius XI, in 1931, that "the right ordering of economic life cannot be left to a free competition of forces. For from this source, as from a poisoned spring, have originated and spread all the errors of individualistic economic teaching."[2] But consider the statement of Pope John Paul II who, in 1979, while strongly condemning exploitation, nevertheless spoke of "...the sector of trade, where the laws of healthy competition must be allowed to lead the way."[3] Is there a contradiction? No, because the first statement refers to the exploitative competition which occurs where freedom is lacking, whereas the second explicitly specifies "healthy competition".

Even so, it may be urged by moralists, competition encourages selfishness, for each party is trying to gain at the expense of other people. Again, I think the notion of one-sided - that is, spurious or exploitative - competition is at the root of the objection. If I gain through possessing an unfair advantage, this may involve selfishness. Suppose I belong to a profession which has been able to restrict its members to below the free market level, and the scarcity enables me to overcharge. That is selfishness. But under conditions of genuine competition selfish acts become more difficult to do, because the other parties have the power to resist the selfish designs I may try to perpetrate. In these circumstances, if I am more successful than my competitors, it is probably because I give better service.

Apart from the ethical question, economic objections are urged against the proposition that competition should be allowed full scope. Let us look at some of these.

Objection 1. Competition leads to monopoly, or at least oligopoly. One way this happens is through the ability of big firms to buy more cheaply than small ones; so they can charge lower prices, which will tend to force smaller competitors out of business. Or they can sell at a loss until their competitors with less financial resources are driven out, then raise prices to recoup the losses. Again, take-overs, especially of firms already struggling because of the practices just mentioned, result in domination by a few large firms. All these tricks are carried out in the name of competition, and if attempts are made to interfere, the firms demand the right to compete freely.

The trend towards monopoly is intensified by the very character of modern corporations. J.K. Galbraith, in his book *The New Industrial State*,[4] examines what he calls the technostructure - the organisation of those who effectively run the large corporation. Embracing all who bring specialised knowledge to the firm's decision-making, the technostructure will serve its own interests, even to the detriment of the shareholders' interests, by, among other things, expanding the corporation's size and by vertical integration to gain control of the whole production process, from the supply of raw materials to the provision of retail outlets.

Reply. The objection implies the goodness of competition. For it is given to show an alleged bad effect of domination by big firms: the crushing of competition. It argues, in effect, that a good thing - competition - will be used to destroy itself. The objection also fails to distinguish between true and spurious competition.

There are factors favouring the smaller firms, including the greater flexibility they often have. A large organisation is likely to find it harder to change direction in response to the market, a principal reason being the difficulty of overseeing and coordinating a vast business network. Regarding the buying power of large firms, referred to in the objection, a practical method for small firms can be the formation of buying cooperatives.

The tendency to monopoly is due in part to defects in the economic system. An example is the way takeover bids are encouraged by taxation rebates allowed on interest payments for money borrowed to finance takeovers. Under a healthy system, we will show later, businesses would be free of the burden of taxation. So this advantage to a takeover predator would simply not exist. Big businesses often have other discriminatory advantages through legislation, such as tariff protection, which allow them to dominate. The solution is to remove the privileges so that genuine competition can flourish.

George Gilder reviews the spate of takeovers in the United States in the 1970's, highlighting the part played by inflation and taxation. These two factors caused investors to pull out of the stock market, causing prices to fall. Then takeovers multiplied. Companies "had no reason to endure the risk and expense of building and equipping new facilities if they could buy existing plants more cheaply."[5] He states that "...the government's very own policies caused some twenty-one hundred corporate merger and acquisition announcements in 1978 alone."

Education must play its part. When corruption is rife, and people are unsure what a healthy economic order is, cynicism and indifference grow. With a better understanding in the community, organisations engaging in spurious competition would find public opinion against them more strongly than today. They would then be less inclined, for example, to try the device of selling at a loss with the aim of driving the opposition out of business.

If, despite all this, large companies prevail over small in some industries, the reason may be that they are more efficient and serve the public better. Their size need not be a matter for concern, granted that the defects just discussed are dealt with. They will each compete for a share of the market, and each will be aware not only of the actual competition of the others, whether local or overseas, but of the potential competitors waiting to enter the market if higher profits make it attractive.

Objection 2. Competition sometimes leads to higher prices through encouragement of the proliferation of small firms, which in turn means that economies of scale are reduced.

Reply. In addition to the comments already made about the competitiveness of small organisations, we can observe that the problem of higher prices, if it occurs, will be solved by the free market. If big firms are best, taking prices and other factors into account, they will thrive.

Objection 3. Competition is not always practicable. The character of the activity is sometimes such that a few big firms will inevitably dominate the market. The automobile industry is an example. Or the railways - it would be ridiculous to have two railways serving the same region!

Reply. In situations where competition looks impracticable, pathological conditions may be the culprit. We must realise (and this will become clearer in the chapters to follow) that our economy is a blend of the natural and the unnatural, which gives rise to unhealthy combinations that may look inevitable in an advanced industrial society. They sometimes originate in the domination of natural resources, as by a few major oil enterprises.

As mentioned, even when only a few firms operate, competition may still prevail. But what of a single railway serving a region? Can there be competition? Yes, because the service is the transportation of people and commodities. But this can be done by other means. So the railway does have competition, which will sharpen if its prices rise or the quality of its service falls.

Objection 4. If unrestricted competition for work is allowed, some workers will suffer. For unrestricted competition would presumably mean no basic wage, no minimum award wages, no right to picket. All these, surely, are restrictions on competition: they prevent employers from acting as they wish, are so many hindrances to the freedom of employers. And what of strikes? Are they not a form of coercion opposed to the operation of the free market? Doesn't a doctrine of unrestricted competition require that they be outlawed?

Reply. The advocacy of these measures to protect workers derives its force largely from the existence of the spurious competition analysed in the previous chapter. It is because of the lack of opportunities to pursue alternatives that people may be forced to work for a pittance. So attempts are made to balance the situation by legislation, by strong unions to take on powerful employers, and so forth. The basic solution, then, is to promote conditions that will ensure the diversity of opportunities essential to true competition, conditions discussed in the previous chapter. But what of the concrete situation where due freedom is lacking - where true competition is not operating? What is to be done while these are absent?

The concept of relative violence is pertinent here. Suppose a doctor prescribes cortisone for a patient. The cortisone has two effects: it acts against the illness and it acts against the patient's health. In the first way it aids health; in the second it diminishes it. Its adverse effect on the human organism is an act of violence: an act against the nature of the human body. And if this were its only effect it should not be prescribed. But the illness which it counters is, the doctor judges, doing worse violence to the patient than the cortisone. The treatment is justified on the grounds that a relatively violent act is needed to prevent greater violence.

The same principle has to be applied in the case we are discussing. Granted an unhealthy state of society, with many workers deprived of the conditions necessary for true competition to function, relatively violent measures will be needed until that situation can be remedied.

Minimum wage legislation may be needed. Some free market advocates will disagree, pointing out that unemployment results from minimum wage laws, as there are always people who cannot earn the legislated wage. Three further consequences studied by R.B. McKenzie are a fall in on-the-job training; fewer workers given fewer hours to do the same work; a big reduction in fringe benefits.[6] I concede the disadvantages. Certainly the setting of minimum rates should be at a level which will exclude few would-be workers. But given the existence of groups of workers in a weak bargaining position, they will often be forced to take less than they are really earning unless some form of relative violence is used to redress the situation. For this reason, too, strikes may be the lesser of two evils when economic conditions are unjust.

Objection 5. Unrestricted market freedom brings chaos in the allocation of resources. This applies to the use of scarce raw materials, to the kind of goods to be produced and the quantities needed, to the application of capital and to the training of personnel. Concerning the last point: quotas may be necessary - in medical schools, for instance, so that the market will not be flooded with doctors in the years ahead.

Reply. Analysis of the pricing system in a free market provides the answer to this objection. It will be dealt with in the next chapter, and is of such vital importance that economic science cannot be understood without it. Briefly, the interaction of millions of individuals and firms, each seeking particular objectives, gives rise to a market where desires are satisfied far more effectively than could possibly be done by any attempt at overall planning; and this is achieved through the action of freely determined prices. By contrast, one has only to look at the former Soviet Union to see the economic disaster of more than seventy years of central planning.

The objection speaks of the alleged need of quotas. But the free market way of dealing with a possible oversupply of workers in a particular field is, firstly, to make as much information available as possible, so that those contemplating a certain career can decide whether there is likely to be enough work in the future. Secondly, the greatest practicable flexibility in changing one's occupation should be allowed. But let the individuals decide, not the planners through a quota system.

Suppose it looks as though there will be an oversupply of doctors, judging by the number of current medical students. This indicates that the medical profession is seen as more attractive than alternatives. The increase in the number of doctors, if free enterprise is allowed to function, will reduce their pay to a level where the socially required number is attracted to the profession. A quota system, on the other hand, is a method of keeping their pay above what it should be. It is a device to allow overcharging. Planning results in the promotion of sectional interests. Lobbies and other pressure groups proliferate, and it is not the weakest but the strongest who benefit most.

Objection 6. Modern research is very costly, often requiring teams of investigators, a long period of time and expensive equipment. Big firms are better able to undertake the research, and the benefits accruing to all may outweigh restrictions on competition.

Reply. Firstly, if this advantage does exist, it still needs to be shown that it is preferable to the evils from the restriction of competition. Secondly, when many firms are active there is an impetus to greater initiative in the development of ideas - competition is good here too! Thirdly, there can be common research facilities. And if it be objected that competing firms would be unwilling to cooperate in research, it must be remembered that in an economy where free international trade exists, the threat of innovations from other countries provides a motive for promoting common research facilities.

Various objections to competition relate to international trade, so let us look at some of those.

Objection 7. It is important for a country to develop its industries, but there can be massive obstacles. The same industries already established in other countries, with a large market, and able to economise through the volume of their sales, will have a strong advantage. Their staff will be experienced, whereas the infant industry will have less experienced personnel. In view of these facts, the government should ban or restrict the relevant imports, or impose a tariff high enough to equalise matters.

Reply. This argument does not apply to the usual state of affairs, as the industries which ordinarily clamour for protection are not infant industries. They are large and experienced. It is a fact of life that governments are induced to give protection by political muscle rather than by real or apparent economic necessity; and infant industries don't have much muscle.

The argument from inexperienced personnel is weak, as they can benefit from foreign experience, or from bringing in experts.

As for not having established markets, there is the counterbalancing factor that they are new in the field and people like to try the products of a new company.

While their small volume of sales initially may mean a higher cost of production, this will not necessarily be so. The infant industry has the significant advantage of being able to start with the most modern machinery and, if it learns from established firms elsewhere, the most efficient methods. Often a long-established organisation, having purchased expensive equipment in the past, will retain it as long as possible, even when it is becoming inefficient.

In the case of underdeveloped countries, the basic reason they have trouble starting manufacturing industries is that they are simply not ready for that stage of development. They often lack transport facilities, have inadequate resources for repairing technical equipment, and lack capital. Unjust social structures and political oppression may impede them for a long time from reaching the desired stage. "The greatest disservice the Marcos administration did to the country," says Filipino economist Bernardo Villegas, "was not its plunder of the national treasury. The worst thing they did was to discourage and eliminate entrepreneurial activities."[7] In addition, they sometimes have trouble selling internationally precisely because of the protectionist policies of other countries.

Objection 8. Cheap imports from poor countries are the result of cheap labour. If allowed freely into a nation with high living standards, they will drag wages down.

Reply. On the contrary, cheap imports will tend to improve our living standards. The best position would be to receive goods for nothing! And the next best would be to have slaves working for us! We would get more goods with less outlay. If we think of our total goods and services as a cake to be divided among us, the effect of cheap imports is to increase the size of the cake. That means a larger share will be available for each person. Certainly injustices may occur in the cake's distribution, but that will happen despite the size, not because of it; and restrictions on imports, by reducing the cake, will tend to worsen the plight of the poor.

The idea that cheap imports will lower the level of wages arises from confusion between the effect of cheap imports and the effect of cheap workers. The tendency of cheap imports is to raise the standard of living, whereas the tendency of an influx of workers prepared to accept lower wages is to lower the standard of living of the nation's workers.

Restrictions on free trade contradict the economic common goods of the saving of effort, abundance, and leisure. They make life harder. Adam Smith points out that the tailor does not make his own shoes or the shoemaker his clothes, but each specialises; and, "What is prudence in the conduct of every private family can scarce be folly in that of a great kingdom. If a foreign country can supply us with a commodity cheaper than we ourselves can make it, better buy it of them with some part of the produce of our own industry employed in a way in which we have some advantage."[8]

Objection 9. The lifting of protection will bring unemployment. If a nation's motor industry is heavily protected, for instance, the removal of the protection means a flood of imports and a consequent reduction in the quantity of locally made vehicles, which results in many thousands of workers losing their jobs.

Reply. Jobs will be lost and hardship caused by the sudden elimination of protection. But the situation envisaged is one arising from a pathological state of affairs. It is like that of a drug addict needing to come off drugs, yet with the prospect of suffering as he adjusts to a normal way of living. The argument does not show that protection, *per se*, keeps up employment. It only indicates that the change to a free trade status will involve temporary dislocation. This can be alleviated by making the changes progressively; and retraining programmes should be readily available. Dislocation will be reduced to the extent that competition is operative, with the diversity of opportunity that constitutes its hallmark.

The apparent cogency of the argument comes in large part from fixing one's attention on an easily seen effect of the removal of protective measures - namely, unemployment in the industries concerned - and failing to see the wider consequences of protection. The truth is that while protection allows more employment in certain areas, it reduces it in others. R.B. McKenzie relates the results of the Reagan administration putting a tariff on steel imports in 1984. The aim was to increase employment in the steel industry. By 1986 employment had climbed by 17,000. But employment in steel-user industries fell by more than 52,000, due to higher prices caused by the tariff.[9]

Protection also reduces employment in other areas by leaving people with less to spend. If they got things cheaper (the things they buy from the protected industries), they would have more to spend; and when most people have more to spend, they spend it. So more production, and therefore more employment, would be generated where the spending took place.

Another way in which protection restricts employment is in keeping down the level of exports. Without protection more would be imported, and consequently more would be exported to pay for the imports.[10]

Objection 10. Military defence requires limitations on competition. If vital industries succumb to import pressure, the country could find itself at the mercy of hostile nations, through lacking the capacity to produce the military supplies it needed.

Reply. This is an extra-economic reason for limiting competition, a reason based on the presence of an abnormal, but only too common, reality: the danger of domination by other nations. Faced with that evil situation, actions may be necessary which would be wrong under healthy conditions. It is another case of the principle of relative violence. Even in the matter of defence, however, special assistance might not be required. But if it is, protection of the relevant industries must be strictly limited to what is necessary. Further, the end should be achieved by direct subsidies to the affected industries, not by discrimination against imports. In this way the price of imports is not increased; the precise effects of the aid can be more easily seen; the public can know what they are paying, and to whom.

To sum up. Anita M. Benvignati rightly states: "An overwhelming conclusion in the economics of international trade is that free trade yields the greatest welfare gains to all participating nations."[11]

A Reminder: the Meaning of Competition

It is perhaps helpful to remind ourselves of the sense in which the word competition is being used in this work. It was defined: **Economic agents, all with a diversity of opportunities open to them, striving through exchange to provide or obtain labour, wealth or services.** It is not equivalent to what economists call perfect competition, nor to various other senses in which the word is sometimes used. It is related to man as a being of intellect and will who aims to possess commodities with a saving of effort, and to have leisure for non-economic activities. Competition is a property of freedom, in the sense that it flows inevitably from freedom - taking freedom as meaning the possession of a variety of choices, a "diversity of opportunities".

Given the liberty to choose among many alternatives, each of us will tend to choose what best suits our needs and is the most efficient and satisfying use of our abilities. If each person has that power of choosing, each can resist domination by those who would selfishly try to get what they want at the expense of others. It is the powerless - those who lack a variety of opportunities - who are vulnerable.

Granted true competition and the elimination, as far as possible, of the spurious competition where some have freedom and some lack it, the common good will flourish. People will be more contented, for they will not labour under conditions that oppress them while benefiting their oppressors; abilities and resources will be used to the best advantage; each will find that serving others through the market is the best way to further one's own interests.

References

1 David Ricardo,*The Principles of Political Economy and Taxation*, London, Dent, 1960 reprint, chapter 5, p. 61.
2 Pius XI, Encyclical *Quadragesimo Anno*, n. 88.
3 John Paul II, Encyclical *Redemptor Hominis*, section 16.
4 J.K. Galbraith, *The New Industrial State*, Boston, Houghton Mifflin, 4th edition, 1985.
5 George Gilder, *Wealth and Poverty*, New York, Basic Books, 1981, p. 176.
6 R.B. McKenzie, *The American Job Machine*, New York, Universe Books, 1988, p. 238.
7 Bernardo Villegas, *Economics and Society*, Manila, Sinag-Tala, 1989, p. 6.
8 Adam Smith, *The Wealth of Nations*, London, Dent, 1960 reprint, book IV, chapter 2, p. 401 (volume 1).
9 R.B. McKenzie, *ibid.* pp. 148-149.
10 See Henry Hazlitt, *Economics in One Lesson*, Connecticut, Arlington House, 1979, p. 77.
11 Anita M. Benvignati, "Barriers to Trade", in *The McGraw-Hill Encyclopedia of Economics*, editor in chief Douglas Greenwald, New York, McGraw-Hill, 1994.

5

The Function of Prices

The price system is central to the economy; is the nervous system of the economic order. Price is the supreme directive and dynamic force, both coordinating and moving the economy.

We state the price of something when we say how much it will exchange for. Often the word is used of the money-price, the amount of money a thing will bring; but it refers also to the quantity of other commodities obtainable for the thing. It is the measure of the value of one thing compared with another. It can therefore be defined: **The quantification of value**. An alternative definition is: **The measurement of relative command over human exertion**, a definition to be examined later in dealing with the concept of value.

Learning from the Pencil

In seeing how the price mechanism works, let us start by looking at an ingenious article called *I, Pencil*, written by Leonard E. Read.[1] The account is supposedly by a lead pencil detailing its own development; and perhaps the pencil's most fascinating statement is this: "Not a single person on the face of the earth knows how to make me."

The pencil then explains the meaning of its assertion. It mentions the tree from which it came, the variety of tasks and equipment required to harvest the logs, the construction of railroads for transport, the series of processes to fashion the slat of wood that will become the pencil, and so on. Then there are the other ingredients: lacquer, printed labelling, graphite, metal, eraser. All these, similarly, result from a series of processes and activities. Each person occupied in the work of making the pencil contributes only a tiny bit of know-how to the finished article. Some may even be ignorant of what a pencil is. Nor do they make their contribution because they want a pencil; they do so to exchange the result of their efforts for other things they want.

34

One might be tempted to think that the enormously complex activities necessary for the making of a pencil would require a master planner who would consciously coordinate the efforts of the multitude of people participating. A moment's reflection shows this is not so, yet people tend to assume that in a complex society there is need for comprehensive planning. Perhaps in a small community, it might be thought, economic life could be allowed to grow without deliberate, overall planning; but in a complex society that would be utterly impossible. To attempt it would be to cause chaos. However, the lesson of the pencil - that it was produced without a centrally directed plan - points to the correct answer. It is precisely when economic affairs are most complex that planning is most obviously impossible. If the production of a pencil cannot be the result of a consciously directed plan, *a fortiori* a whole economy cannot be planned; and the more complex and far-flung the economy, the more ridiculous the attempt to plan it.

The Price Mechanism at Work

How, then, does a harmonious economic society arise? What cause explains it? The answer has already been indicated: the price mechanism. Since each person wants to satisfy desires with economy of effort, the worker wants a high price for labour and the investor for investment, while the consumer wants to pay a low price. Prices, therefore, are an inducement or a deterrent, pulling economic activities in this or that direction. But they are not pulled haphazardly: the shape which emerges will reflect the desires of those participating, given the prevailing circumstances. That last phrase is important: oppression, for instance, can result in people desiring something they would shun under more favourable conditions. A worker may desire back-breaking labour for a low wage because the alternative is starvation. On the other hand, genuine competition will operate, through the price system, to bring equitable results.

It is only when prices are determined by a truly free market that the economy will function well, for prices coordinate production, and the process will be distorted when prices are interfered with. As Milton and Rose Friedman explain,[2] prices coordinate production through the three functions of transmitting information, providing incentives and distributing income. Let us examine those functions, comparing what happens in a free market with what happens when there is interference.

Transmitting information. When demand for an article increases, the higher price that results is a signal to the market that a greater quantity is wanted. The price mechanism ensures that the right people get the information, and that they are not overwhelmed by facts they do not need. Those interested in particular prices will be on the look out for changes, and will ignore prices they are not interested in. Pencil manufacturers, for instance, know the suppliers of wood, and are aware of current prices and of prices for future delivery.

When one sees the importance of the information-transmitting function of prices, it becomes clear that harm will be done by anything that distorts them. But distortion is inevitable when price regulation occurs, whether done by the government or the private sector, because to regulate prices means to change them from what they would be if left alone, and thereby to alter the information transmitted. Distortions will occur if the government imposes a maximum price on an article, or imposes tariff laws, or grants subsidies. Likewise, inflation interferes with price signals: it becomes hard to judge whether a price rise is a signal to produce more, or whether it is simply an effect of inflation.

Providing incentives. Prices not only show where action is needed, but give an incentive to those in a position to act. If the price of wood rises because of greater demand, the rise is an incentive to wood producers. Not only that, but it provides the means of producing more. It may be necessary, say, to offer higher wages to get the extra workers who are needed, and the increased price provides the means of paying them. Moreover, there is an incentive to act in the most economical way - to avoid waste. So if resources are scarce (a situation signalled by higher prices), those using them will be led, by the higher prices, either to be more careful in their use or to find alternatives.

The evil effects of price interference appear with sharp clarity in relation to incentives, causing an imbalance between supply and demand. Suppose the government tampers with the market price by granting a subsidy to producers. This is an excessive incentive: excessive in relation to the quantity that would otherwise be produced. It tends to bring about a glut. An opposite effect, in regard to price incentives, is found when minimum wages are legislated and the amount is above what the market is prepared to pay. As Gregory Mankiw states: "The government causes wage rigidity when it prevents wages from falling to equilibrium levels."[3] Employers will not subsidise less able or less experienced workers, so these people will struggle, prevents wages from falling to equilibrium levels."[3] Employers will not subsidise less able or less experienced workers, so these people will struggle, often in vain, to get a job. The incentive for a firm to employ them is just not sufficient. It is no coincidence that as minimum wages for juniors have risen compared with other wages, their relative level of unemployment has also risen. The tragic fact is that legislation, interfering with the price mechanism, has priced some out of the labour market. Mankiw continues: "The minimum wage is often thought to have its greatest impact on teenage unemployment." Noting that many researchers have studied the question, he says: "These studies find that a 10 per cent increase in the minimum wage reduces teenage employment by 1 to 3 per cent."[4]

Distributing income. In addition to transmitting information and providing incentives, prices distribute income. In fact, the price one receives *is* one's income: the worker receives a price (a wage) for his work, the investor receives a price (a return) for his investment. In a truly free market incomes will be distributed equitably, for those who are dissatisfied with their returns will find an alternative. In this way the problem of just prices is solved, whether it is question of wages, return to investors, or the price the consumer pays. But when a system is riddled with privileges to particular groups or individuals, income distribution becomes unjust.

At times a privilege becomes capitalised on the market, and can be clearly seen. Take egg producers being allotted a quota of hens, which they are forbidden by law to exceed. And egg prices are fixed. The outcome to be expected is that egg prices will be above what a free market would give. How do we know when this is so? By the price of hen quotas: if we find producers being prepared to pay for the quotas, the conclusion follows that there is an excess profit, measured by the amount offered for the quota.

Governments intervene in the distribution process by trying, as they claim, to make it more equitable - to see the less advantaged get a bigger share than the market allots them. Our examination of the price mechanism shows the harmfulness of the practice. It distorts the signals, leading inevitably to maldistribution and disruption. To the extent that distribution is interfered with, incentives will become either defective or excessive and the wrong information will be transmitted. That is why farm subsidies, as in the case of wheat or wool, lead to embarrassing surpluses: a price in excess

To sum up. The price mechanism, if allowed to function freely, transmits the appropriate information needed by economic society, provides the necessary incentives, and distributes incomes equitably. But if interfered with, whether by selfish private interests or (perhaps well-intentioned) public legislation, the result will tend towards chaos and injustice.

Self Interest and the Invisible Hand

Adam Smith spoke of the individual, in endeavouring to achieve his own interests, as at the same time and without realising it promoting the public interest: "…he is in this, as in many other cases, led by an invisible hand to promote an end which was no part of his intention."[5] He observes that "it is not from the benevolence of the butcher, the brewer, or the baker that we expect our dinner, but from their regard to their own interest."[6]

This has been criticised as a canonisation of selfishness, as well as being impracticable in that, it is objected, the promotion of individual interests will not lead to the general interest and a harmoniously functioning economy, but to conflict and fragmentation.

On reflection it is obvious that attention to our own interests may indeed promote the common good. Take marriage. When a couple decide to marry they are thinking of their own good rather than that of society as a whole. If a young man proposed to a girl and offered as his reason, "The promotion of the common good", she would be wise to refuse him. Yet if they marry with their own good in mind, the marriage will still help society's welfare. Similarly, when we choose a certain job rather than something else, we think, generally, of our personal advantage and the good of those close to us, rather than the common good. But if we choose an occupation which suits us, this will probably be more beneficial for society than if we had chosen one less personally suitable. When we like doing something, this indicates we are talented in that direction, and therefore able to benefit the community more than in an occupation for which we have less talent.

Not only are we using our best talents, but we find, in a society where there is true competition, that we best advance our own interests by serving others. Whether working, investing, selling consumer goods, each must supply what others want. Further, self interest leads to each resisting attempts by others to exploit them. It is not in my interest to be exploited or even to get less service from one person or firm than I can from another.

Self interest promotes the common good in all these ways even when the motives of individuals are selfish. Selfishness means an inordinate attachment to one's own interests, with disregard for other people. It tends to the disruption of society, for the selfish seek ways to benefit at the expense of others, and therefore attack the true competition which is essential for a just society. Not only that, but selfishness, even when operating as a motive for serving the community, lessens the quality of the service rendered. Take a shopkeeper who is polite, obliging, aiming always to meet his customers' wishes - but only to further his own interests. Now contrast him with his competitor down the street who is motivated not only by his own interests but by a genuine regard for those of his customers and by a love for the common good of society. The difference of outlook will be apparent to those who know them well, making it more pleasant to deal with the second than with the first; and it will lead the second to do more for his customers than the other, for selfishness does not provide the same motivation to give service.

Self interest does not necessarily mean selfishness; it may be a due concern for oneself. If one wants job satisfaction, a decent living standard, leisure time, one is not thereby being selfish. Nor does special regard for family and friends demand a disregard for the community as a whole.

The harmony of the invisible hand, working through free prices, will be facilitated by a reasonable concern for self and those close to oneself, together with a love for the common good. But even with widespread selfishness, great harmony will still exist, although less than it should be, to the extent that competition allows the free price system to function.

References
1. *The Freeman*, December, 1958.
2. M. and R. Friedman, *Free To Choose*, Melbourne, Macmillan, 1980, chapter 1.
3. N. G. Mankiw, *Macroeconomics*, New York, Worth Publishers, 1994, p. 127.
4. *Ibid.*
5. *The Wealth of Nations*, London, Dent, 1960 reprint, book IV, chapter 2, p. 400, (volume 1).
6. *Ibid*, book I, chapter 2, p. 13.

6

Wealth and Services

The word wealth is used with a range of meanings by economists,[1] for it can refer to things produced by labour; to natural resources; to financial assets such as loans, shares or money; even to skills and other personal qualities that enable one to earn an income. Some elements, including money, will be accepted by one economist and rejected by another. A term embracing so much is too vague, while disagreement as to whether certain elements should be there causes confusion.

Defining Wealth

It is important, therefore, to be clear about the sense in which we are using the word. It is also important to use it in a sense which helps to classify economic facts logically and realistically. Now we can achieve this, as I hope to show, by restricting the word to the sense in which Henry George employed it.[2] It can be defined (and this is the only sense in which I will employ the word in the present work): **Natural resources that have been modified by human exertion to make them fit, or more fit, for the satisfaction of desire**.

This definition expresses the reality in terms of its four causes, in the Aristotelian sense: it gives the matter (the material cause); the specifying element (the formal cause); the productive agent (the efficient cause); the end (the final cause).

Natural resources names the matter of wealth: the stuff it comes from. This is something provided by nature, not produced by man. For example, a box is an article of wealth, and the wood from which it is made is given by nature. *Modified ...to make them fit, or more fit...* indicates the formal cause: that which specifies the thing to be what it is. A box arises from the materials being appropriately modified, until they have the shape and structure which constitutes them as a box. *Human exertion* is the efficient cause: the agent acting to produce the thing. All the workers from the timber cutter who felled the tree contribute to the product by their work, the carpenter who constructed the box being, through his exertion, the proximate efficient cause. *For the satisfaction of desire* names the final cause: the end or purpose of the article of wealth; for instance, the storage and carrying capability of the box.

The modification referred to in our definition is not confined to the changing of the thing's physical properties. It embraces any change giving the article of wealth a greater fitness for the satisfaction of desire. If a commodity is transported from a warehouse to a retail shop, it is thereby given a greater capacity to satisfy desire, for it is brought to a place where it is accessible to the potential consumer. The transportation of an article (its modification according to place) adds to it a further degree of wealth.

Numerous activities usually called services are really wealth-producing activities if we use the word wealth according to this definition. The work of a shop assistant is an example. It constitutes part of the labour required to bring a material thing (such as a packet of biscuits or a radio) to the point of satisfying human desire: it is directed to a modification of the article, as regards accessibility and transference to the consumer. Likewise, in the production of a newspaper it is not only the printers but all those working to put the finished commodity in the hands of the consumer who are wealth producers - including the boy who sells papers on a street corner. Each modifies the newspaper in some way, making it fitter for the satisfaction of desire.

Failure to distinguish wealth from services shows up in the classifications made by official statisticians. One anomaly in the United States pointed out by R.B. McKenzie is the classification of a hamburger sold at a fast-food restaurant as part of a service, while a hamburger sold at a grocery store is a good.[3] If we muddle our terms we will muddle our thoughts.

Wealth is vastly increased by a smoothly functioning market, which ensures that goods and services get where they are wanted - and therefore where they are more fully articles of wealth, for they more perfectly satisfy desire. The production of wealth is not just an individual undertaking, but flows in part from the very structure of society: there is a social production of wealth, over and above the contribution made by each individual, for the social organism enables a product to better satisfy desire.

The words commodities or products or goods can be used to name what we have called wealth; but if we do so it is important to keep in mind that the *modification to satisfy desire* goes beyond the physical characteristics.

If the commodity is a motor vehicle still in the factory, it is less wealth than a physically similar vehicle in a retail outlet.

What of the inclusion of natural resources as wealth? Or work skills and similar personal qualities that enable one to produce more? Or valuable rights such as a taxi licence? Or money?

Natural resources are the matter or stuff from which wealth arises, the basis of wealth. Qualities like work skills pertain to the efficient cause of wealth, namely, the worker. Valuable rights are outside our definition of wealth, but can be confused with wealth because they are a means of acquiring it. The same applies to money, which is essentially a medium in the exchange of wealth; it is not *that which* is wanted "for the satisfaction of desire", to quote from the definition of wealth, but *that with which* we obtain the products, the wealth, we desire. So money taken formally - that is, precisely as money - is not wealth.

What if we take it materially: if we view coins or bank notes as artefacts? In that sense it is wealth. *It is natural resources modified by human exertion*, to fit them for *the satisfaction of desire*. And the desire is to have the benefits conferred by this medium of exchange. Similarly, coin collectors view money materially: they prize the coins as such, and not precisely as a medium of exchange.

Passing to another question on the definition of wealth: Would *enhancement of life* be the correct understanding, instead of *satisfaction of desire*, as the end or purpose? The point of the question is this. Desires are not all of equal value; some indeed are destructive. Are we, then, to assess two products as equally articles of wealth even though one is directed to a praiseworthy desire and the other to a desire unworthy of human beings? If thumb screws are desired for purposes of torture, are they just as much articles of wealth as screwdrivers?

To answer this, we need to remember that only what comes under the principles of economics can rightly be considered by the economist. Suppose an accountant is asked to cooperate in stealing money from his firm, his skills as an accountant to be utilised to conceal the crime. He should make a moral judgment about the proposed action; but he could not do so precisely as an accountant. The reason is that accountancy does not provide the principles needed to assess the moral character of the action. Similarly, we must ask whether the principles of economics provide the answer to the question: Is this article of wealth apt to enhance the quality of life more than that article of wealth? Economics has no principles from which it can answer the question, so it has to stick to a definition of wealth proper to its own field.

Standards beyond those proper to economics must be applied, but when this is done it will not be by the economist formally as such, just as the accountant is obliged to apply standards beyond the scope of accountancy, but cannot do so precisely as an accountant.

The Meaning of Services

We have seen that some activities generally called services are actually wealth producing activities, for they give the article a greater fitness to satisfy desire. We said that the boy who sells newspapers is causing an increase of wealth, just as are the printers who operate the machines. However, there are services which are distinct from wealth.

Think of the labour of a barber, or a bus driver, or a doctor, or a teacher. It does not cause the modification of natural resources - that is, of the non-human environment given by nature. So it does not produce wealth in the sense defined. Yet it does something, and something important. It provides a service, which is: **The satisfaction of desire by human exertion, without the production of wealth**. An alternative definition brings out more clearly the resemblance of services to wealth, yet the contrast between them: **Modification of the person, through human exertion, towards the satisfaction of desire**.

Whereas in wealth production a modification of non-human matter occurs, the provision of a service consists in the modification of a human being. The barber modifies the hair by cutting and shaping it, the bus driver relocates the traveller; the doctor improves the patient's health; the teacher imparts knowledge to the student's mind. But whether wealth is being produced or a service rendered, human exertion is being exercised to cause a modification towards the satisfaction of desire. Not that the person who is the recipient of the service is necessarily the one who desires it. Parents may desire that a teacher educate their child in mathematics, while the child may not like the idea. Nor is the service necessarily for the benefit of the recipient. Just as something can be an article of wealth, yet be detrimental, so an economic service may be detrimental to the recipient. But provided it answers to the desire of the person or persons who sought it, it is a service in the economic sense.

The fact that a service, like an article of wealth, may be harmful to the true good of the persons concerned is of major importance to society. But the economist, *precisely as such*, is unable to assess good and evil that lie beyond economics.

References

[1] See D. Rutherford, *Dictionary of Economics*, London, Routledge, 1992; J.W. Kendrick, *The McGraw-Hill Encyclopedia of Economics*, editor in chief D. Greenwald, New York, McGraw-Hill, 1994.

[2] See his *Progress and Poverty*, New York, Robert Schalkenbach Foundation, 1987 reprint, book I, chapter 2; *The Science of Political Economy*, Robert Schalkenbach Foundation, 1981 reprint, book II, chapter 15.

[3] R.B. McKenzie, *The American Job Machine*, New York, Universe Books, 1988, p. 47.

7

The Science of Economics

We must now deal with these important questions: What do we mean by saying economics is a science? Can economics be considered on two levels, one phenomenal, the other philosophical? Is economics an ethical study - a part of the science of ethics? Does it rest on unchangeable principles?

Defining Economics

Let us start by proposing a definition of economics: **The science of wealth and services, as priced**.

Science. For the moment we can take science loosely as an organised body of knowledge concerning a specific object of study.

Wealth and services. The previous chapter explored their meaning. They are what people seek in forming an economic community. They are therefore the subject matter of economics. Without them no economic system would exist. Yet there can be wealth and services without an economy. A Robinson Crusoe can make articles of wealth, but there will be no economy, for there will be no trade. Wealth and services in an economy are social realities; they exist in a social framework.

Priced. When wealth and services are traded they receive a price. Indeed, only by means of the price system can an economy be maintained. Chapter five discussed how prices transmit information, provide incentives and distribute income. We saw how free prices animate the economy, imparting to it an energy and harmony otherwise impossible to achieve. So it is never merely wealth and services the economist studies, but priced wealth and services. Wealth and services are the matter of the economist's study, but price is the form: it is the specifying and determining element.

The relation between services and price enables us to answer a question about the range of services listed in the economy. Are they all of an economic nature, or are some, strictly speaking, outside the economic order? Take the work of a music teacher. Music belongs to a higher sphere of activity than the economic. In chapter one we classified four social levels: economic, recreational, political, cultural. Economic life is the most fundamental, but man is more than an economic animal. In music, for instance, he shares in a cultural experience. What, then, are we to say of services pertaining to recreation, to politics, to culture? Is the musician or the music teacher a worker in the economy?

The answer might seem to be negative, for the service is in the recreational and cultural orders. However, if the service is priced, would not this bring it into the economy?

We must distinguish between a thing and an object. Water, for example, is a thing, but that one thing can be many objects. The swimmer will view it from one aspect, the fisherman from another, the sailor from a third, the thirsty person from a fourth.

Applying this distinction to our question, the service provided by the musician, or that provided by the music teacher, can be viewed either as it is cultural (or recreational), or as it is the provision of a priced service. In the latter way, and only in that way, it comes under the economist's consideration and is an economic object.

Economics as a Science

Returning to the notion of economics as a science, is it a science only in a very wide sense? Every science supposes order - there can't be a science of chaos. If an underlying order exists, a reliable body of knowledge is possible, but not otherwise. Hence a classical definition of science is: **Certain knowledge through an understanding of causes**. Merely probable knowledge that something is so does not suffice for a statement to be scientific. Nor is it enough to know what happens, while being quite ignorant of the causes. Scientific inquiry seeks the reasons, the causes.

Some say, therefore, that if we call economics a science we are speaking loosely, for it is about the actions of unpredictable human beings. There is really no telling what they will do next.

Two orders: one existential, the other essential. To understand the status of economics, we must distinguish two kinds of order, each with its appropriate kind of laws.

One is the order or harmony found in physical nature: it is an existential order, in the sense that it is actually out there to be observed. The order the astronomer studies is of this kind. But suppose the stars and planets had a will of their own and could arbitrarily change their movements. Then there might be chaos instead of order. The astronomer might have to give up in despair, unable to construct a body of scientific knowledge because the subject of study was a collection of random occurrences, not an intelligible order.

In human affairs, unlike physical nature, harmony is interfered with by individuals making arbitrary choices. But this does not mean there is no order of any sort. For some choices are right in the sense that they promote social and individual good, others are wrong in the sense that they attack this. So the former are in accord with what we can call an essential order; that is, they are in line with what human nature requires for its fulfilment. And economics deals with this order.

Just as physical nature is harmonious through the operation of determinate laws, e.g. the law of gravity, economic society is harmonious through the operation of laws based in human nature; but because we are capable of choosing to act against these laws, the harmony found in practice is greatly diminished. Somewhat similarly, if the planet Mars could choose to flout the law of gravity, the present harmony of the solar system would be disrupted.

There is a natural economic order, but it is natural in the sense that it harmonises with, and is demanded by, man's social nature. It is a blueprint for healthy economic life; so it is constituted by nature. But it has to be instituted or implemented by society's members. To make this clearer, we can look at some of the laws which, I maintain, are natural, and essential for the healthy functioning of society.

One is the principle of subsidiarity: **What can be done by an individual or smaller group should not be assigned to a larger group**. We argued that it is based in human nature, for man has intelligence and free will, and should therefore be allowed all reasonable scope for initiative. Hence the functioning of the principle will promote the good of the person and of society, whereas ignoring it will tend to frustrate both.

True competition is another principle or law required for a healthy economy. Flowing from the same reality of human nature, and greatly aided by the principle of subsidiarity, it ensures an equitable distribution of rewards and the best provision of wealth and services.

It does this through the operation of free prices, which are a property, or inevitable consequence, of subsidiarity and competition. So these three principles or laws - subsidiarity, competition, a free price system - are natural in the sense that they flow from human nature. Beings of intelligence and free will are oriented to these in their economic life; and consequently are frustrated to the extent that the principles are not operative.

These and other principles (including the vitally important matter of the distribution of site revenue, yet to be discussed), make the economy a naturally ordered system. But all these laws can be flouted; and in greater or less degree they are flouted in existing economies. So it is clear that the order we are examining is an essential order: it is what ought to be; but is not an existential - actually existing - order, except imperfectly.

What, then, of the word science in our definition of economics? Specifically, is it science in the classical sense of **certain knowledge through an understanding of causes**? From what we have been saying the answer can be reached. It is clearly not a science in the sense that physics, for instance, is science, because it does not deal with an actually existing order. However, science is wider in meaning than that, as when one speaks of the science of ethics; and economics viewed from the philosophical standpoint taken in this book fits the definition.

It is about an *understanding of causes*. We have just spoken of four realities fundamental to the subject. There are others, including the principle of the saving of effort, and the common good of the abundance of wealth and services. These are based in human nature considered individually and socially, with its powers, its needs, its desires. They are not confined to some periods of history or to some societies, but are common to all times and societies. Therefore in proceeding from these realities the discipline of economics is about an *understanding of causes*. And because the causes are stable they give us knowledge that is certain, not merely probable. So economics, in the sense in which I am using the term, is a true science.

Two levels: philosophical and phenomenal. My standpoint is a philosophical one. That is, throughout this book I am viewing economics as an intelligible harmony based in human nature, although achieved only imperfectly in actual life.

But this is not the viewpoint of most economists. They are concerned rather with analysing the economic phenomena confronting us, without delving into the question of *what ought to be*. They are primarily interested in how people and society *choose* to behave in organising production and consumption. They study factual situations, suggest ways of achieving goals, predict outcomes. They will explore the level of unemployment, the percentage of various groups out of work - youth, the unskilled, rural workers, and so on - the length of time the unemployment has lasted, the means taken to remedy it. But study of the phenomena may be aimed at getting the facts without resolving them into fundamental principles.

This is the level at which most economists work, and it is essential that the work be done. The trouble is, the deeper level is neglected, which makes it impossible to have a sound understanding of economic society, for the unchanging laws (unchanging because rooted in human nature) which should regulate economic activities are ignored.

To sum up. There is a level of investigation which studies phenomena, and which can be called empirical or positive economics. There is another level which studies primarily the fundamental natures underlying the phenomena, and can be called philosophical economics. The first is basically concerned with what is, the second with what ought to be.

Empirical economics has less title than philosophical economics to the name science, for it is less occupied with viewing things in the light of causes. Not that the two are separate; they are two approaches to the study of economic society, and in practice tend to merge. Both, in fact, study phenomena, but philosophical economics does so with the explicit aim of understanding the unchanging realities manifested by the phenomena. In examining, say, the effects of price control, it will seek, through these effects, to see whether free prices are natural.

Economics and Ethics

How is economics related to ethics? Most economists would say it is something other than ethics. According to Murray Rothbard, the economist should realise "that economics can establish *no* ethical principles by itself - that it can only furnish existential laws to the ethicist or citizen as data."[1] Likewise, P.E. Kennedy, although he distinguishes between positive and normative economics, sees the normative element as coming from outside economics,[2] with the politician, citizen or ethician applying non-economic principles to economic data. An example would be a proposal to introduce improved machinery rapidly, when conditions were such that unemployment could be expected to result. Moral principles from outside economics should be applied to the economic facts, to arrive at the right decision. Karl Popper speaks similarly of physical science. "No amount of physics will tell a scientist that it is the right thing for him to construct a plough, or an aeroplane, or an atomic bomb..."[3]

Empirical economics is indeed a non-ethical discipline. It is true too that moral principles have to be applied in the way described. But in the case of philosophical economics, while the application of extrinsic moral principles must be done, there is this essential difference: philosophical economics is a part of ethics or moral philosophy. For ethics (moral philosophy) is a study of how man ought to act. But philosophical economics studies how man ought to act in the economic field, for it is about an order which is natural to humanity, and whose implementation will bring justice, while its neglect will bring injustice.

It is only a small part of ethics, confined as it is to natural *economic* laws. It cannot even tell us how we should use the leisure it promotes. Nor can it distinguish morally between different articles of wealth: it cannot say whether tomatoes are better than thumbscrews. It can't do so because these moral evaluations depend on principles outside the economic order, and therefore economics is blind in their regard. Nevertheless it is linked with all of ethics - and with philosophy as a whole, with psychology, and with other disciplines.

However strange it may seem to most modern economists to say that fundamental economics is a department of ethics, when we look at the history of economics we find philosophers and theologians to be the first in the field. In ancient Greece Plato and Aristotle treated economic questions in their examination of ethics. Medieval and Renaissance philosophers and theologians did the same - a fact brought out clearly in A.A. Chafuen's work *Christians for Freedom*.[4] Among the first to establish economics as a distinct discipline, the physiocrats saw it as the study of a natural moral order, while Adam Smith taught it as Professor of Moral Philosophy.

Today, too, philosophers, theologians and religious leaders deal with economic questions. They are not stepping outside their field, given that economics, in the sense explained, is a part of social ethics. Whether they are competent to deal with it is another question! The efforts of some are pathetic, showing little or no awareness of basic principles, such as the system of free prices, and typically ending with an appeal for government intervention.

The Nobility of Economic Science

E.F. Schumacher makes the disparaging comment: "No doubt economists of whatever philosophical persuasion have their usefulness at certain stages of development and for strictly circumscribed jobs."[5] Others would go further, and see economics as mercenary, although something that cannot altogether be dispensed with; but certainly lacking nobility.

It should instead be seen as the study of a marvellous order in human affairs. Economic life is the fundamental part of that great whole which is human society; and a true grasp of the way the economy ought to operate shows it as a thing of harmony and beauty, every part cooperating for the common good, and its inherent laws distributing benefits equitably. All the other activities of the society - recreational, cultural, political - depend on the economy, somewhat as all the activities of a human being depend on the basic nutritional functions. Without satisfactory nutrition the other functions, including those engaging the highest exercise of mind and will, are going to be weakened and distorted. Similarly, in society, the further an economy moves from its proper order, the greater the maladies at every level of the social body.

Poverty will obviously prevent, often in a tragic degree, the flowering of the human potentialities of those afflicted by it. Uncongenial labour, due to lack of the opportunities that should be available to every worker, can mean years of bitterness and sadness, with little prospect of an improvement until retirement allows one to escape from the labour force. Again, injustice in the economy's functioning brings the corruption of its perpetrators and a strong pull for people who would otherwise be honest to be drawn into dishonest practices in, as it were, self-defence. Structural injustices in the economy generate enmity where there should be friendship among the members and classes of society.

Many worry about the encroachment of the state on personal freedom, and various proposals are advanced to dismantle public undertakings, or to provide safeguards for freedom. But given a natural order, no satisfactory remedy exists except the implementation of that order. To act against it is to do violence to nature. If, for instance, competition is the natural way of regulating prices, but is not allowed to function, a disorder is present, and any attempt to cure it by government price control will do further violence to the natural order. It is utterly different from the situation where no natural way exists, as in a traffic law that says vehicles must keep to one side of the road. No natural law tells us to keep left, or to keep right; so a human decree that we must do one but not the other isn't a violation of nature.

It is hard to repress nature. That is why a black market arises when the free market is repressed. So we find a struggle by the natural order to assert itself, while governments - and special interest groups - adopt repressive measures to maintain violent arbitrary arrangements in opposition to nature. Inevitably, if the true order is missing, there will be interference with personal rights and excessive government intervention.

References

[1] M. Rothbard, *Power and Market*, Menlo Park, California, Institute for Humane Studies, 1970, p. 101, original italics.
[2] P.E. Kennedy, *Macroeconomics*, Boston, Alleyn and Bacon, 1975, pp. 13, 409.
[3] Karl Popper, *Conjectures and Refutations*, London, Routledge and Kegan Paul, 1962, p. 359.
[4] A.A. Chafuen, *Christians for Freedom*, San Francisco, Ignatius Press, 1986.
[5] E.F. Schumacher, *Small is Beautiful*, London, Sphere Books, 1974, p. 141.

8

Labour and Wages

Work, Wealth and Toil

Labour, or work, in the economic sense, is: **Exercise of human activity in production**.

It is *human*. A machine is said to work, but strictly it is the human being who works, using the machine as an instrument. Work proceeds from the person, who is central in economics. The *activity* constituting work or labour may be intellectual or physical. "Labor comprises the broad category of human effort, both physical and mental. Labor includes the effort of both the cab driver and the brain surgeon."[1] Economically speaking, the director of a business empire is a labourer, for he is doing essentially the same as a ditch digger; namely, exercising human activity in production. Nor is the labour of the ditch digger merely manual or physical; no human work is, for intellect and will always play a part. By *production* is meant: **The process of satisfying human desire through the provision of wealth and services**.

Wealth is produced by the application of labour to natural resources. This is done in three ways, which have been called adapting, growing and exchanging.[2]

Adapting covers all those acts of production which consist in making use of natural resources that are already present. Mining, oil extraction, fishing, brick making, converting trees into lumber (and the further stages right up to the construction of houses or furniture): all come under the heading of adapting.

Growing is the raising of living things, whether flora or fauna. Its distinctive mark is the utilisation of the powers of growth and reproduction peculiar to living things, by which an increase of wealth is achieved.

Exchanging, or trading, is the specifically social way of producing wealth. In chapter two, dealing with the common good, we saw that people can do far more when working together than the same number could do in isolation. But this is effected by exchanging. Because each is able to exchange what he produces, each is able to specialise, making use of his particular aptitudes (which also tends to give more enjoyment than work for which one has less aptitude), and developing greater skill through specialisation. Likewise, the advantages resulting from trade with other places are made possible by exchange.

If I am a farmer and produce potatoes, then exchange them, through the medium of money, for a table and some chairs, I am using my powers, under the impetus of the principle of the saving of effort, to gain articles of wealth that I want. The carpenter, on his side, is doing the same. I can produce potatoes more easily than tables and chairs, whereas the reverse applies to the carpenter. So through the exchange each of us is better off. The very exchange itself has caused an increase of wealth, as we see clearly on recalling the definition of wealth given in chapter six. It means the giving of fitness, or greater fitness, for the satisfaction of desire. But the potatoes on the one side, and the table and chairs on the other, are made more fit for the satisfaction of desire through being exchanged, since each of us gets what *he* wants by exchanging what he does not want.

Exchange, therefore, not only makes possible all the advantages of specialisation and so on, not only makes the existence of the economic order possible, but also increases wealth through the very act of exchanging goods we desire less for those we desire more.

Comparing the three modes of production: adapting uses qualities inherent in all material things; growing uses qualities proper to living things; exchanging uses a quality proper to the human race - the ability to trade, derived from reason.

Permeating all three modes is the activity of the human spirit as the radical source of wealth. Michael Novak declares: "...of all the resources available to any nation, its material resources are less important than the minds and habits of its citizens. The sources of creativity lie in the spirit of invention, discipline, and order."[3]

Labour and toil. The proposition that work or labour is good would be thought dubious by some workers, in view of their daily difficulties and the weariness from forty hours or more a week on the job, as well as the crowding out of things they would rather be doing. Admittedly it is good in the way unpleasant medicine is good - as a means to an end: the provision of the commodities and services the worker produces and the acquisition of commodities and services through his wage.

But this is not the only way labour is good. It also often gives pleasure to the worker, for it is normal to derive pleasure from the exercise of our powers. Further, it provides opportunities for enjoyment, as in the companionship of one's fellow workers. And it is usually good in the sense that it is a fitting use of human faculties, an activity that develops one's skills, even one's character.

Yet we know well there is another aspect to labour, an unpleasantness that looms large in the estimation of many workers. This aspect is brought out by the word toil, which signifies the arduousness, the strain, the monotony found in work. Under the heading of toil we can place any unpleasantness or inconvenience, including the exclusion from more pleasant or more fitting activities. Employment always has an opportunity cost: the exclusion from things one would rather be doing.

So work is good, but toil is bad. Admittedly, even toil may be good in the sense of being useful for attaining something good, as when one's character is strengthened through the difficulties encountered in work; but bad personal effects occur too. The object should be to reduce toil, and the extent to which this is done is an index of how well an economy is performing.

Is it implied there should be less work? Yes; especially because of the opportunity cost: making a living excludes one, to some degree, from doing other things. Leisure, as we have seen, is a common good at which the economy aims. While economics cannot tell us what to do with leisure, a larger view of human nature than economics provides shows us higher pursuits to which time should be given. Aristotle says wisely that "Nature herself...requires that we should be able, not only to work well, but to use leisure well...Both are required, but leisure is better than occupation and is its end; and therefore the question must be asked, what ought we to do when at leisure?"[4] Leisure from earning a living is leisure for better things.

The Payment of Wages

Let us analyse this definition of wages: **Recompense for effort expended in production**.

The word effort covers every aspect of the toil or arduousness or unpleasantness of work. These make it less attractive, so (other things being equal), a higher wage is needed to induce workers to offer their services.

Contrariwise, the more pleasant the work, the less reluctant people will be to engage in it.

However, we must take a longer look at the notion of recompense for effort, since a glance at actual situations shows that people are often not adequately compensated for effort. The reverse often seems true: the jobs with the most effort or toil, the most unpleasantness, are the low paid ones. Sometimes the rejoinder is made that the higher paid occupations usually require a longer period of training, and that the pay is, in part, compensation for this. Certainly that is a factor, but it is often overrated, for many students in the professions find their period of training enjoyable and do not need the incentive of such a high return as they expect to receive on completion of their studies.

Take two extremes: the position of a slave and that of a sinecurist. In the worst degree of slavery, the slave will be at subsistence level, with no regard for effort expended. The goods doled out in return for work are the equivalent of the upkeep of a draught horse, and no more deserve to be called wages then would the food and amenities given the horse. At the other extreme, the sinecurist is paid well although doing little work, and again there is no relation between the payment and the effort. In these extreme cases, is a wage being paid? Surely we are diluting the meaning of the word if we use it where the notion of reward or compensation or recompense is absent. Hence the slave at subsistence level can hardly be said to receive a wage, and the greater part of the sinecurist's payment, while it may be a gratuity or even a bribe, is not a wage, because not a recompense for effort.

Payment for effort - or for products and services? The objection may be raised that wages are not paid for effort, but for products and services. Suppose I want fly screens for the windows, and get quotes from two handymen. One of these men really enjoys his work and finds it easy, whereas the other dislikes his work and finds it difficult. Also, the first is faster than the other, although just as efficient. Then each gives a quote which represents payment for the amount of effort he honestly thinks the job will entail. And one quote is twice as high as the other! Well, there's not much doubt which I will choose. As with consumers generally, I will be interested in the product, not in the degree of toil undergone by the worker - even if I could gauge this.

It is true that the consumer pays for products, but equally true that wages are related to effort. While the consumer does not base his buying decisions on the toil associated with producing the goods, the worker has this criterion in choosing a job. That does not mean the individual worker can tailor his wage to his toil. What it does mean is that, through competition, a social wage will be paid which reflects an assessment by the workers as a whole of the degree of toil associated with the work, and after allowing for positive elements, such as enjoyment of the work and pleasant company. The principle of the saving of effort, which operates in all areas of life and in every person, ensures that the workers will seek a wage that compensates for the toil. As a result, competition will bring about a situation where payment varies from job to job according to the relative effort which workers as a whole judge it to involve.

It is of the utmost importance to see that the adjustment will be imperfect to the extent that true competition, as examined in chapter three, is lacking. If, for instance, a large section of the population is poorly educated, the range of job opportunities may be too restricted to allow proper freedom of choice.

Where competition is seriously impaired, the main cause is the economic malady we have named privilege, and which we defined: **A power accorded by the state to some, with undue discrimination against others**. It may operate indirectly against a decent wage, as when it has resulted in a poorly educated class who, consequently, cannot compete. Or it may operate directly, allowing powerful interests to gain unfair advantages. If the effects of privilege could be eliminated, so that all classes of workers had a wide range of opportunities open to them, the universal desire to save effort would adjust rewards to the degree of toil undergone by the average worker.

Justice through competition. The concept of a just wage is important in social ethics, and suggestions are offered about ways of achieving it. Unfortunately, the recommendations are often in terms of government intervention. The idea that there might be a natural solution is ignored by many ethicians. Yet there is such a solution, and it consists in the functioning of true competition - which will come spontaneously if privilege is removed. Certainly there will be anomalies, but they will not be a major problem. Cases will always exist where individuals are unable to stand up for their rights, and other cases in which individuals are in a position where few can compete with them - top tennis players, for instance, who may, as a result, receive payments far in excess of their efforts. Or scarcity of a skill may result, for a time, in higher than normal payments.

But the implementation of competition, primarily through the elimination of privilege, is the natural way to wage justice.

Given the variety of opportunities implied by competition, and if this state of affairs flourished throughout society, we would find workers in the less attractive occupations receiving far more than they do now; while those in the currently higher paid professions would often get relatively less. Not that all the coal miners would become lawyers; but there would be a sufficient movement away from mining, and a sufficient movement into law, to bring relatively higher wages for the one compared with the other.

References

1. William A. McEachern, *Economics: A Contemporary Introduction*, Cincinnati, South-Western Publishing Co., 1994, p. 3.
2. See Henry George, *The Science of Political Economy*, New York, Robert Schalkenbach Foundation, 1981 reprint, book III, chapter 2.
3. Michael Novak, *This Hemisphere of Liberty*, Washington DC, American Enterprise Institute for Public Policy Research, 1990, p. 50.
4. Aristotle, *Politics*, book VIII, chapter 3, 1337b, 30-34.

9

Capital and Interest

Examination of Capital

We are faced again with an over-worked term: capital. In a wide sense it is used of "...any asset or stock of assets - financial or physical - capable of generating income."[1] I am using the term more restrictively.

Definition. Capital in that sense is: **Wealth employed as an instrument of production**. This names something having a unique place.

We defined *wealth* as: **Natural resources that have been modified by human exertion to make them fit, or more fit, for the satisfaction of desire**. So capital consists of products: things on which labour has been bestowed.

An *instrument* is something made use of by a principal agent. Here it is products used by workers. Tools, machinery, vehicles obviously come under this heading. Slightly less obviously, so do buildings, for they contribute to the efficiency of the work, as by making conditions more comfortable and by protecting goods from the weather. Considerably less obviously, although it should be seen from the notion of wealth, capital includes products on the way to the consumer, right from the initial stages of production up to the point of sale. The reason is that wealth is caused or increased by modifying natural resources towards the satisfaction of desire - including, as we saw, modification according to place, as when goods are transported from a warehouse to a shop, making them more accessible. "Fitness to satisfy desire" is increased by moving an article from the warehouse to the shelves of a store. The article, therefore, is being used as an instrument in generating an increase of wealth when transported and placed on the retail shelf. Hence the stock yet to be sold forms part of the capital of the owner, just as do lathes, trucks, factories, and other instruments of production. The production of wealth continues while ever further utility, or fitness to satisfy desire, is being added to the goods.

The word *production* embraces the provision of services. A bus used for public transport is not an instrument in the production of wealth, but of a service, namely the relocation of people from one point to another.

The purpose of capital. As the economy exists to provide more wealth and more leisure with less effort, this too is the purpose of capital. Suppose a producer were considering buying a more expensive machine than the one currently in use, but found after investigating its possibilities that it would not alter the level of production. He would not buy it, as there would be no gain.

The benefits of capital are immense - perhaps their very immensity conceals them from us. But imagine what life would be without capital. Were it completely lacking, we would be forced to exist (if we could exist under those conditions) by gathering what nature offered, in so far as it could be done with our bare hands. Even a flint knife or a bow and arrow are capital. Think of the factories, warehouses, office blocks, shops; the roads and railways; the planes, ships, motor vehicles; the vast array of tools and machinery; the stocks of goods awaiting purchasers: all this capital makes possible the consumption goods we so casually take for granted.

P.T. Bauer comments: "In Africa as elsewhere in the Third World, the most prosperous areas are those with most commercial contacts with the West."[2] Prosperity usually diminishes, he points out, as one moves away from the impact of the West.

Capital has enabled the West to prosper, and to improve living standards elsewhere. Emulation of Western methods has furthered the process. Despite the evils which have accompanied the process, the benefits of capital in the Third World should be acknowledged, and are a striking confirmation of the value of capital.

Investors are great and irreplaceable benefactors of the human race. Whatever their personal motives, they are providing an essential means to the living of a civilised life.

Despite all this, the worker is the principal cause in wealth production, capital remaining always but an instrument. This primacy, and the relation between the two, are obscured if we talk, as economists sometimes do, of "human capital", meaning qualities like education which enable the worker to perform more efficiently. In that sense Paul Samuelson says: "When you see a medical-school graduate, you are in a certain sense looking at a chunk of capital."[3]

But can't capital be destructive and dehumanising? A producer may choose to install "soul-destroying" machinery which tends, due to monotony, or noise, or danger to health, to dehumanise the operator. This has often been the case (classically in the early industrial period), and it still happens. The worker is being treated as a tool, like a piece of capital, instead of a human being. Such abuses will occur when true economic competition is impeded. Otherwise the operator would presumably refuse the work unless the wage were so high that he judged himself adequately compensated.

What of the claim that capital destroys jobs? After all, the whole point of capital is to reduce work. This too can be an acute problem in the absence of competition, whereas the flexibility and opportunities of competition will minimise the difficulty. Also, work will result from the capital, possibly even in the very occupations where new capital seems a threat, for lower prices may bring higher sales; but particularly because the savings generated by the capital will leave people with more to spend elsewhere.

Spurious capital. If someone buys a taxi, and the price of the licence plate alone, after the cost of the vehicle and equipment, is $A250,000,[4] what is being bought? The cab itself, with its fittings, is capital: an instrument in the production of a service. But this is not true of the plate. Yet it constitutes the major cost. In this instance a monopoly right is being bought. The plate is priced at that level because of the benefits the buyer can expect through the restricted entry into the business caused by the licensing system. In conditions of free entry, competition would ensure that there were either cheaper fares or more taxis available at the same fares.

At first glance it appears that a genuine capital investment has been made, but this is not so, for the $250,000 has not purchased wealth to be devoted to production. It has purchased a power to charge a higher than competitive price to consumers.

Another example of the practice is the takeover of a firm for a sum that would be excessive, only that it eliminates a competitor, and therefore allows higher prices to be charged. A third example is the price of a seat on the stock exchange.

Our economic system is riddled with this type of "investment", merged with real investment in capital goods. Thus we have a schizophrenic system, where low prices are being caused by true capital and simultaneously impeded by spurious capital. The basic difference between the two is that capital produces wealth, and therefore earns an income (interest), whereas spurious capital is produced by an income. In the examples, an income is available because of restrictive practices, an income above that which competition would allow. It is then capitalised. So the $250,000 for the taxi plate is not capital, but the capitalisation of an excessive income.

An ironical element is that the recipient often receives little benefit, because the seller charges a price that captures the estimated benefit. With the taxi plate, the buyer does not get a better return on the outlay than would be obtained from an investment in capital goods. (And the driver gets no benefit.) However, there is consequently a stronger incentive for the buyer to push for a greater degree of privilege from the government, as this will bring a bigger gain. Thus privilege breeds further privilege.

Spurious capital can be defined: **Capitalisation of an unearned income**. It is the antithesis of true capital, which is productive, whereas spurious capital is anti-productive. Note that it is not merely non-productive, but is essentially an impediment to the production of wealth and services. It is therefor an enemy of the economic common good, an enemy of the economy's *raison d'être*.

The frequent use of the word capital in a sense so wide that it includes even spurious capital should alert us to the danger of using terms in a way that obscures reality instead of manifesting it. How can we think clearly if a key word, like capital, is employed to name opposite things?

Interest, or the Return on Capital
By interest is meant: **Recompense for the investment of capital**. The word is often used for the payment on consumer loans, but there is this big difference: capital produces a return, whereas consumer goods do not. If I buy a truck to carry goods commercially, I will expect the activity to yield a return on my investment. If I buy a car for personal use, there will be no return.

The users of capital are willing to pay interest because the capital *causes* the wealth from which interest is paid. A business man thinking of installing a new machine calculates whether sufficient will be earned with the use of the machine to cover the cost of the capital. If he invests wealth he already has, he will want a return commensurate with what he could obtain by investing it elsewhere. If he borrows, he will want to cover his interest payments.

But is a return on capital a just recompense? Karl Marx denied that it is, maintaining that the investor does nothing to earn it.

Abstinence is one reason advanced in defence of the investor's right to a return. By abstinence is meant the forgoing of present consumption. A present good tends to attract us more than a future good: a motor car now rather than in five years' time. But the investor is forgoing consumption goods he could have now. Therefore, it is argued, he is rightly compensated by being paid interest.

While the principle of the argument is true (a present good does tend to be more attractive than a future good), the supposition is that other things remain equal. But suppose I want to buy a car or a house or some other expensive commodity for which I lack the funds at present. The desire for the commodity might be a sufficient motive for me to save, even though no interest were offered. Again, the very possession of capital (and of funds lent for the buying of consumer goods) is an attraction to some. It brings a sense of security, even a sense of power. So the satisfaction derived from investments may fully compensate for the abstinence from present consumption. However, abstinence remains a factor in the justification of interest, for it is often not cancelled out by other considerations.

Liquidity preference is another factor. According to John Maynard Keynes the principal explanation for interest is found in the desire to have funds available. People are prepared to tie up their funds only if an incentive, namely interest, is offered. He defines interest as "the reward for parting with liquidity for a specified period."[5] He says: "Thus the rate of interest at any time, being the reward of parting with liquidity, is the measure of the unwillingness of those who possess money to part with their liquid control over it."[6] There are obvious disadvantages in tying up one's funds, such as the possibility that they will be needed sooner than anticipated, or the risk of missing out on a better investment at a later date.

Despite this, Henry Hazlitt gives figures to show that short term rates for borrowed money in the United States were as often above as below long term rates between 1865 and 1958.[7] So we need to be cautious about the argument. One point is that people sometimes deliberately tie up their money for a long term because they know they are tempted to spend it when it is readily available.

In discussing the justification of interest, inflation and taxation must not be forgotten. People complain about, say, a fifteen per cent return on an investment, and claim it is usurious. But suppose forty per cent of that goes in taxation and fifty per cent is eaten up by inflation. The net return is not fifteen per cent; it is one and a half per cent.

Should the investment be risky, compensation for the risk must be allowed, and a high gross return may represent a low net return.

As with other prices, the rate of return on investments should be determined by the market. If a relatively high return occurs in one sphere, an influx of investors attracted by the high rate will force it down. If a relatively low return is being paid, investors will go elsewhere, and the rate will rise. In this way, funds will flow to where they are most wanted. We saw in chapter five that prices function, when not impeded, to transmit information, to provide incentives and to distribute incomes. It applies to all prices, including the return on investments; and the chaos resulting from attempts to interfere with the natural mechanism occurs also when interest rates are manipulated. The wrong signals are given, resulting in resources being badly employed.

Complaints are made that, because capital and borrowed funds are scarce, investors receive an inequitable return. The criticism comes partly from neglecting to notice the effects of inflation and taxation, and concentrating on gross instead of net returns. Surely a return of one and a half per cent could hardly be called inequitable, yet the solid and trouble free investments criticised for their high returns often yield no more.

Still, rates would be lower if more funds were available relatively to demand, for supply and demand are the proximate determinants of price. And more funds would be available if it were not for causes resulting principally from faults of the government.

One is the spurious capital analysed above. It absorbs funds that would otherwise be available for productive purposes. Think of the enormous amounts paid out by home buyers because of the cost of land. It will be shown later that land price is a form of spurious capital and that there is a remedy for it. Clearly, if this expense could be minimised (as it could), more funds would flow into productive investments.

The level of borrowing is artificially high because of the encouragement given by taxation deductions on interest payments, diverting funds from other uses. Then there are the huge amounts borrowed by governments. Also, interest rates are often stimulated deliberately by government manipulation.

There was a time when the Bank of England and the Bank of France paid depositors nothing on funds at call;[8] people found sufficient incentive in the convenience and security afforded. This is an indication of the extremely low rates that might prevail on relatively risk free investments if artificial causes did not increase the scarcity of funds and reduce the net return.

References

1 Bannock, Baxter and Davis, *Dictionary of Economics*, London, Penguin, 1987.
2 P.T. Bauer, *Equality, the Third World and Economic Delusion*, Cambridge, Massachusetts, Harvard University Press, 1981, p. 70.
3 Paul Samuelson, *Economics*, New York, McGraw-Hill, 1967, p. 48.
4 This is an advertised price, in Australian dollars, for an unrestricted cab licence plate in Sydney. See *The Sydney Morning Herald*, 23 March, 1996, p. 73. They can be leased for $400 and more per week.
5 J.M. Keynes, *The General Theory of Employment, Interest and Money*, London, Macmillan, 1974 edition, p. 167.
6 *Ibid.*
7 Henry Hazlitt, *The Failure of the "New Economics"*, Lanham, University Press of America, 1983 reprint, p. 450.
8 Charles Gide, *Political Economy*, London, Harrap, 1914, p. 418.

10

The Importance of Land

Economists employ the word land in a wider sense than its everyday meaning, to embrace not only the surface of the earth, but the whole natural environment in which man lives and works. It includes the sea, mineral deposits, flora and fauna, even sun, wind and other requisites and aids to human life and work. As William A. McEachern says, it represents "…all so-called gifts of nature, including bodies of water, trees, minerals, and even animals."[1]

It is particularly in relation to production that land is studied in economics, and from that standpoint is: **Natural resources, excluding human activity**. It is all the basic resources - such as minerals, timber, fish and land animals, sun, air, the fertility of the soil - used to produce goods and services.

But as the word is also used to embrace the terrain on which we live, its meaning in that wider sense is: **The natural environment, excluding human activity**. As we have said, man is not simply an economic being, but has numerous activities, including the most important, outside the economic order. Land is needed for these too. It is needed for recreation, for cultural activities, for merely living. It is appreciated for its beauty.

What is meant by saying that natural resources (or the natural environment) are considered as excluding human activity? The point is that land is not produced, but is something given, something that is there to start with. It is that upon which and with which we work, not anything made by us. The making of a chair can be traced back from the final touches to the finding of the tree that would be felled to provide most of the material. But when we get back there we are confronted with a primary source; and it is a source independent of, and presupposed to, human labour. Or think of the growing of a wheat crop. The labour exercised in that work supposes seed, suitable soil, water, sunlight, air. The farmer can help nature, as by providing fertilisers or installing an irrigation system; but there must be basic natural resources that were given and not made. All human production of goods depends on pre-existing material. These unproduced resources, and the whole unproduced environment, are called land, in economic terminology.

Samuelson and Nordhaus remark: "While land can sometimes be created by drainage or landfill, land usually cannot be augmented in response to a higher price or diminished in response to a lower price."[2] However, what happens in these and similar cases is the application of labour and capital to land, resulting in a product. It is not simply land we finish with, but wealth. Land as such cannot be made. The distinction is important, for it enables us to distinguish in our thought what is distinct in reality. Then we see more clearly the nature of wealth, defined earlier as: **Natural resources that have been modified by human exertion to make them fit, or more fit, for the satisfaction of desire**. Land (natural resources) is the matter, the material cause, of wealth.

Perhaps it is advisable to add that distinction is not separation, for it means "lack of identity", whereas separation means "lack of union". My two hands are distinct from each other (one is not the other); but if I join them they are not separated - they are united.

Among economists Henry George saw more clearly than any before him, and almost all after him, the distinction between wealth and land. "The essential character of the one class of things is that they embody labour, are brought into being by human exertion, their existence or nonexistence, their increase or diminution, depending on man. The essential character of the other class of things is that they do not embody labor, and exist irrespective of human exertion and irrespective of man; they are the field or environment in which man finds himself; the storehouse from which his needs must be supplied; the raw material upon which and the forces with which alone his labor can act."[3]

Land provides a space to live and work: space in which to exist, to move about, to pursue our various activities, to store products, to construct buildings. Land is the storehouse and quarry from which we obtain the materials we use; those materials which form the indispensable basis of every piece of wealth we produce. Land also facilitates transport, as when rivers and the sea are used, but above all it helps us through the growth of living things. As the eighteenth century physiocrats clearly saw, nature labours along with man in agriculture. The vital power of growth in living things is used by the farmer in the production of crops and the raising of animals, a power that continues to operate even while the farmer sleeps, and which is so prolific that we might almost be tempted to overlook the struggles and toil of the farmer, and think that nature was doing all the work. Without nature (land) there would be no food and therefore no life.

A further benefit of land is its beauty. The mountains, the sea, the forests; even a single tree viewed through our bedroom window: these delight us and ennoble our sentiments. This quality, although largely beyond the economic order, has its economic aspect, for beauty adds to the price of land.

Mark Twain (or was it Will Rogers?) said of land: "They don't make it any more." Unlike products, land is in relatively fixed supply. It does increase in the sense that flora and fauna increase, but the area of land is not increased, although it can be made more useable, as by drainage, and can be used more intensively, as when a skyscraper is erected.

This inelasticity of supply, in sharp contrast to the supply of goods and services, has profound consequences regarding land prices. If an upsurge occurs in demand for television sets, the price will rise, inducing a greater supply, followed by a reduction in price. The supply can be increased at will, for television sets are produced by human effort. But this does not apply to land, so a greater demand leads to a price increase without the remedy of an increased supply. The ramifications will be studied later.

Another consequence of the fixed supply relates to conservation. For land can be diminished, whether in quantity or quality. Minerals are depleted by mining and oil drilling. Hunting and fishing can deplete animal species to the point where they are in danger of extinction. Indirectly the same is possible through urbanisation. Vegetation, too, particularly forests, may be drastically reduced, even to the extent that land becomes barren and deserts encroach on previously fertile terrain. Pollution is another danger to nature, destroying living things and striking at the quality of the environment, including the air we breathe.

Because land is not a product, and therefore cannot be replaced like a machine or other products, particular care needs to be taken in its conservation. On the other hand, nature is extremely prolific and very efficient at replenishing itself - a fact not given enough attention by some conservationists. Those who call constantly for government intervention to solve alleged environmental problems must present strong evidence that the problems are indeed serious. The place of governments will be addressed in chapter seventeen; for the present we can note that society has many prophets whose anticipated calamities are based on emotion rather than reason. Some people even talk as though we were servants of nature, when in reality nature is our servant, for beings of reason and will transcend the whole material universe.

References

[1] W.A. McEachern, *Economics: A Contemporary Introduction*, Cincinnati, South-Western Publishing Co., 1994, p. 3.

[2] P.A. Samuelson and W.D. Nordhaus, *Economics*, New York, McGraw-Hill, 1995, p. 243.

[3] Henry George, *Progress and Poverty*, New York, Robert Schalkenbach Foundation, 1987 reprint, book VII, chapter 1, p. 337f.

11

Association and Site Revenue

Association

We have commented, especially in chapter one, on the benefits bestowed by society. Each person is aided by others, and there is handed on through time the accumulated skills, knowledge and wisdom of the centuries. Thus it is that a person of mediocre ability and knowledge is yet so superior to the level a potential genius would reach if isolated from human contact that he would appear by comparison to belong to a vastly higher species. This is made possible by *association* or *cooperation*, in the sense of **the union of many people to a common end**. Without this, civilisation would not exist.

We are particularly interested here in the economic benefits of cooperation or association.

Suppose a man with great physical strength and an aptitude for every kind of work, whether mental or manual. Suppose he had devoted himself, as though exclusively, to each branch of every trade and profession, and had kept up to date in all of them, developing his skills by constant practice. Imagine the wealth he could produce! But the situation in the real world is similar, because of the division of labour. Without this each person would have to spread his labour over numerous tasks, for many of which he would have little aptitude, and for none of which could he develop the skills and knowledge that come from long practice. However, the specialisation arising from the division of labour causes a result similar to our imaginary all-round worker. Millions of specialists unite in the production of wealth and services.

Add to this the vast savings found in economies of scale, with large quantities being manufactured at a fraction of the cost per unit that a small quantity would incur. There is also the immensely more productive use of capital when the funds of thousands of investors are pooled for capital goods that would otherwise never exist because of their cost.

Through association we achieve, to a degree we rarely pause to think of and are scarcely able to grasp, the common benefits for which the economy exists: the saving of effort, abundance of wealth and services, leisure. These in turn provide the opportunity for cultural activities, which also, as noted, are promoted through association.

To really see what association is, one has to see that society is far more than the sum total of the individuals composing it. Compare it with the human body. If the body were thought of as so many pieces - two arms, two legs, one heart, thirty-two teeth, and so on - it would not be seen realistically. It is more than the sum of its parts; it is an organism. Likewise, a million people existing and working in isolation are not the equivalent of a million forming a society. Confining ourselves to economic concerns, the whole production of the million in isolation, if heaped together, would be a miserable amount compared with that of the million working together. Society, including economic society, is not a collection of individuals, but a social organism, bearing an analogy to that physical organism which is the human body. It is a union of diverse parts united by a common end, a common purpose.

Through association the common end is sought and achieved (although the achievement in practice will always fall short of perfection). Association, therefore, is the unique way of gaining the common goods of the saving of effort, abundance of goods and services, leisure for other activities. The three basic factors of land, labour and capital are enhanced and permeated by association, which marvellously transforms their productiveness.

Association and land. The common good caused by association is closely linked with land, which provides the space in which to live and work. Since association is a social reality, it is more intense and productive where there are more people. Association exists in a small village, but far more in a great city, particularly in the case of economic association, for trade is carried on principally in large centres of population. It follows that people there are able to share more fully in the benefits of economic association, while those on the fringes of society share to a far less degree.

Compare this to a large lecture hall, with people near the front being able to hear the speaker clearly, while those at the back are unable to catch all the words. When the lecturer expresses an idea it is able, from its nature, to be possessed by any number of people. The lecturer will still possess the idea, while giving it to others. But there will be a difficulty due to the location of some listeners, hindering them from fully possessing the idea. It is similar with land. We saw, especially in chapter two, that society generates benefits which are common in the sense that, from their nature, they can be possessed by any number of people. But their possession can be hindered by one's location. If I have a business in a large city, I will participate more in the economic common good than I would in the suburbs; and I would participate more there than in a remote village.

Yet these are *social* benefits: they are produced by society, not by land. The land simply gives access to them. But this is not true of all the benefits afforded by land. There are properties like good soil, mineral deposits, rivers suitable for transport. A beautiful view, especially from a residential site, is a prized benefit.

So we find two distinct kinds of advantage given by land: social benefits and benefits intrinsic to land. But even the latter kind are activated by society, which makes possible their actualisation or fuller actualisation. Gold is no use to a castaway.

Site Revenue

If one piece of land gives higher benefits than another, people will be prepared to pay more. Classically this is called rent, which Adam Smith defines: "The price paid for the use of land."[1] But here we have another terminological problem, for the word rent is used in a much wider sense both in ordinary language and in current economics.

It can mean the income received by the owner of a durable thing, whether land, machinery or some other durable. In economics it can also mean the payment for a factor in excess of what would be needed to keep it in its present employment.[2] Top opera singers are an example of those whose payment is mainly rent, for most of them would be willing to continue in their occupation for a fraction of their present income.

As with other words in economics (wealth and capital are instances already cited), rent is used so broadly that reality is obscured rather than clarified. In view of this, the expression *site revenue* is better, and is the term I will generally use. My use of the word rent in this work is always synonymous with site revenue.

Rent or site revenue means: **Return from situational advantages**. It occurs in four ways.

1. Situational advantages may actually produce the return. A farm with excellent soil and enjoying good rain will cost more because of these advantages; but the advantages will cause greater production, which will pay the cost. Likewise a shop in a prime location will be expensive to buy or

lease, but the benefits of association will cause greater production and pay the cost.

One site may be so poor that the production there is barely enough to cover wages and a market return on capital; which means there is no site revenue whatever. This is marginal land. Another may lease for $50,000, and a third for $500,000. The return is a measure of the assistance given by the site; it is a differential return.

Therefore the revenue from productive sites is: **Return efficiently caused by differential situational advantages**.

The efficient return is the cause that makes something (as explained in chapter six). The return we are interested in here is produced by the advantages of the site, namely advantages conferred by nature and (usually of far more importance) those conferred by human association.

2. The second of the four ways in which there is a return from situational advantages pertains to land not used productively; principally residential land. Someone searching for a suitable home site will want benefits in three categories: (a) intrinsic qualities of the piece of land, such as a moderate slope - a flat block might get water-logged, while a very steep one would be inconvenient; (b) extrinsic physical benefits, like a beautiful view; (c) benefits provided by society, like good roads, shops, recreational and cultural opportunities.

These benefits, varying from site to site, will bring a larger or smaller return when the land is leased or sold, just as for productive land. But with this difference: the return is not produced by the site advantages - they are not its efficient cause. Whereas a business can expect the advantages to generate the rent, the user of residential or other non-productive land must have an outside source from which to pay the rent. Yet in some way the advantages do cause the rent. They cause it in the sense that they are effectively desired by the occupant or potential occupant. In philosophical terminology, they are the *final cause* of the revenue.

The final cause, or end, or purpose, is the thing aimed at, the thing wanted. When we say, "Love of adventure caused him to climb the mountain", we are speaking of a final cause: we are stating the purpose for which the action of mountain climbing was done. And when we say the advantages of which we are speaking are the cause of site revenue, we mean they are that which, by being desired, cause the payment of site revenue.

This form of rent or site revenue is: **Return finally caused by differential situational advantages**.

3. There exists what can be called monopolistic rent. Suppose a man owns the whole of an island and that the inhabitants are unable to migrate. Site revenue will vary from site to site, as it does everywhere. But the owner is an unscrupulous individual who wants as much as he can possibly squeeze from the unfortunate tenants. So he proceeds to charge even for land too poor to have yielded rent previously, having returned only wages and interest. The occupiers will now be forced to accept a lower standard of living. But it will not end there, for the owner's policy will be felt by all on the island, as the rack rent at the margin forces up rent at the higher levels. The result will be a layer of site revenue affecting all land, in addition to the differential revenue corresponding to the degree of advantage one piece of real estate has over another. Monopolistic rent is not a differential return; it is not based on the peculiar advantages of the particular site. It is based on what can be extracted because of a scarcity of land. In the case of our imaginary island, the extreme limit will be fixed by what is required to live at subsistence level. The islanders will be, in effect, slaves of the landlord.

These dire consequences suppose the islanders powerless to emigrate or resist. But even in the freer conditions prevailing in the real world, some degree of monopolistic rent exists. It occurs when land is so scarce that what would otherwise be marginal land has to be paid for. It can happen through zoning laws limiting the land that can be put to a particular use. Or population pressure may result in monopolistic rent. The land of Japan in 1988 was valued at more than the combined land of the United States, Canada and France.[3]

This form of site revenue can be defined: **Return irrespective of differential advantages**. It is extracted as a condition of using advantages common to all the sites in question.

4. Finally, there is speculative rent. This comes from the anticipation of increased benefits in the future. For instance, in a progressive society it is to be expected that greater benefits will attach to land in the coming years. So sellers will price their land to allow for the anticipated increase, and buyers will be willing to pay extra for the same reason.

Site revenue of this kind is: **Measure of the return expected from future situational advantages**.

There is a risk factor, because the hoped for returns may not eventuate. As will be seen later, speculative site revenue is a major cause of economic slumps.

Usually a leaseholder does not pay the speculative element in rent, as he will be willing to pay only for the advantages he will actually enjoy, not for those anticipated after the term of the lease. The land owner alone pays for those.

Briefly, speculative site revenue is an element added to natural site revenue, and does not represent a return presently attaching to the land, but the anticipation of a future return. The claim that it is unnatural will be defended in the next chapter, after the foundation has been laid.

The following schema summarises the various modes of site revenue.

Rent
- in common: Return from situational advantages
- specifically:
  - in production: Return efficiently caused by differential rent situational advantages
  - outside production: Return finally caused by differential specifically situational advantages
  - monopolistic: Return irrespective of situational advantages
  - speculative: Measure of the return expected from future situational advantages

References

[1] Adam Smith, *The Wealth of Nations*, London, Dent, 1960 reprint, book 1, chapter 11, p. 130.

[2] See, e.g. Donald Rutherford, *Dictionary of Economics*, London, Routledge, 1992, under **rent** and **economic rent**.

[3] See Fred Harrison in *Costing the Earth*, edited by Ronald Banks, London, Shepheard-Walwyn, 1989, p. 17.

12

The Government's Natural Revenue

The benefits for which site revenue is paid are from physical nature and, especially, from society. This indicates the right recipient of the revenue.

Site Revenue Belongs to Society

Benefits freely bestowed by nature are there for the whole community, while social benefits are caused by the community. It follows that they belong to the community, not to individuals. Compare it with wages. If I work to produce a commodity, I am the one who should be paid, not some bystander. And the same principle applies to what the society produces: society should be the beneficiary. Individuals have no entitlement to appropriate these social benefits for themselves.

Buying the common good. The conclusion is clearer if we recall the concept of the common good. A common good is generated by society, and is apt, from its nature, to be possessed by any number of people without being diminished.

However, in locations which give greater access to it than others, people get more of society's common good. If I own a piece of real estate in a thriving commercial centre, I will share far more in the benefits society provides than a business person a hundred miles away in a small town. I may operate a business myself, or lease my site; in either case I can expect wealth to pour in - not in payment for what I have provided, but for what society has provided. If I own a piece of land and do nothing with it for twenty years, but social progress causes a vast increase in values during that time, I may become rich; yet my contribution has been nil. Like Rip Van Winkle I could have slept for the whole period, but would still reap the reward for what my community had done.

Examples of how benefits tend to go to land owners, even though meant for others, are provided by a British study made by the Department of the Environment in 1988.[1] The main taxes affecting urban land, the study concluded, were Corporation Tax, the Rates, and Value Added Tax. Concerning the Corporation Tax, the study said: "The lower the level of Corporation Tax, the greater a company's bargaining power in terms of financial resources available to bid up rents in order to secure and retain the premises of its choice. Landlords benefit twice over..."[2]

The study gives examples from the Enterprise Zones, where the government provided grants and tax allowances for capital expenditure and relief from local taxes. "The capital allowance concession increases the rate of return to developers and again tends to feed through into higher land values. The rates concession represents a direct saving to tenants (and owner occupiers) but there is evidence that it is largely offset by higher rental values, which in turn feed through into capital and land values."[3]

The buying and selling of sites, and their leasing, is a buying and selling of the common good.

In chapter nine the concept of spurious capital was discussed. Defining it as **capitalisation of an unearned income**, we saw that it does not produce wealth (as genuine capital does). Now it is apparent that we are confronted, in land prices, with a gross example of spurious capital. If you buy machinery for a million dollars and I pay the same for a piece of industrial land, we may both seem to be making a capital investment, whereas in reality you alone are doing so. You are contributing to society by providing capital goods, which are an instrument of production that increases wealth. I, on the other hand, am buying the right to a favoured share of the common good.

The present land system is an appalling institutionalisation of privilege - that is, of **a power accorded by the state to some, with undue discrimination against others**. The land owner, because of our laws, receives what rightfully belongs to the community. Then, possessed of the power afforded by valuable land, he is able to further infringe the rights of others, as by the edge owner-occupiers often have over competitors who lease premises, and are consequently at a disadvantage, especially in difficult times.

Further considerations. The fittingness of the proposal appears more clearly when we realise that the only alternative to taking this revenue for public purposes is to appropriate private property. The government needs funds, and must get them from somewhere; if not from what the community as such has caused, then from what individuals have earned. But why should we have to hand over part of our property for public purposes when this special source of revenue exists? What justification is there for leaving the latter in private hands and taxing the former instead? The origin of each points unambiguously to its right destination: what the community causes should be its revenue; what individuals produce should be their property, unless the community's proper revenue proves insufficient.

The naturalness of site revenue for public use is also indicated by the fact that the fund increases with society's need of it. In the early stages of society, less government funds are required; and there is also less site revenue. But as society develops, more money is required; and there is also an increase in site revenue.

The system should be introduced gradually to avoid undue disruption, but when fully operative it would involve the government collecting annual revenue from each site having value, the revenue being at a level which would reduce the site's selling price to a small percentage of its present amount. In some countries, such as Australia, the practice of raising revenue from the unimproved value of land is widespread, leaving the improvements untaxed. But because of the low percentage taken, land prices remain high. Were the percentage increased, a point would be reached where land would bring only a small price when sold. That is the situation to aim for.

Is the proposal practicable? I have just sketched its basic rationale, although much remains to be discussed. But at this stage we can draw attention to a psychological difficulty that tends to block a fair assessment. The difficulty arises whenever a theory is presented whose acceptance would involve a major adjustment in one's thinking. We don't want to change our accustomed way of viewing the matter - perhaps don't want the effort of changing it. We also tend to an uncritical acceptance of the status quo, although often unwilling to admit it. Then there is the influence of experts (or alleged experts), whose judgment is against the theory. Selfishness can warp the mind too, as when we suspect, even if wrongly, that we would suffer from the introduction of the controversial idea; or perhaps from supporting the idea when most of our peers reject it.

All these pressures exert their influence on many who are faced with the concept under examination here, and the pressure can be so strong that the concept is either rejected without a fair hearing, or consigned forever to the "too hard" basket. We must be on our guard against the pressure, and make the effort to look impartially at the facts, regardless of whether they are popular or otherwise. Not that the proposal is novel, nor is it without strong historical antecedents.

During the Middle Ages, and to some extent in ancient times, land holding was seen as necessarily bound up with service to the sovereign and to the community. Medieval land owners were expected to provide fully equipped soldiers when required by the sovereign, and to maintain roads and administer the laws. Revenue from lands owned by the Church was used for education and for care of the sick and the poor. There were extensive commons: land for everybody's use.

Among economists, many have advocated the public use of land revenues, including Adam Smith and the physiocrats in the eighteenth century. The physiocrats especially insisted on it, seeing the rent of agricultural land as the natural source of state funds. They proposed an *impôt unique*, or single tax, as the correct way of financing government needs.

Smith points out advantages of ground rent (revenue from land alone, excluding buildings and other improvements). "Ground-rents are a still more suitable subject of taxation than the rent of houses. A tax upon ground-rents would not raise the rent of houses. It would fall altogether on the owner of the ground-rent..."[4] He goes on to say that the taking of ground rent does not discourage any sort of industry. Further: "Nothing can be more reasonable than that a fund which owes its existence to the good government of the state should be taxed peculiarly, or should contribute something more than the greater part of other funds, towards the support of that government."[5]

The outstanding exponent of the position that the state should take the ground rent was Henry George (1839-1897). In fact, he is usually remembered for this alone, although he put forward a system of political economy, especially in his book *The Science of Political Economy*. He viewed site revenue in its full amplitude; not just as a return in agriculture - a restriction found in the physiocrats. And he perceived clearly that the benefits bestowed by society are its main source.

George's influence was enormous, especially through his book *Progress and Poverty*, which has sold millions of copies and has been translated into many languages. But from professional economists he encountered far more opposition than support, and was often surprisingly misunderstood - and still is. Professor Mark Blaug observes that "all the leading British and American economists of the day...wrote extensive critiques of George. As R.V.Andelson...makes clear, the story is one of persistent misunderstanding, misrepresentation and downright evasion of the issues by the leading members of the economics profession."[6]

Nevertheless, the question of revenue from land remains a much discussed topic. In his article in *Land Value Taxation*, Mason Gaffney shows the range of interest from economists and assessors, and comments: "It would be hard to find a topic on which so many economists have rendered opinions and taken positions over the last two hundred years."[7]

In the United States there is a strong trend towards reducing taxes on buildings and taking site revenue instead. Steven Cord, among others, has shown the beneficial effects, and quotes a research monograph of the prestigious Urban Land Institute which describes it as "the golden key to urban renewal - to the automatic regeneration of the city, and not at public expense."[8]

The practice of exempting improvements from taxation, placing a charge only on the land, operates in most Australian and New Zealand local government areas. Professor Steven Cord, analysing the data, particularly for Australia, demonstrates the benefits in terms of greater building activity and higher employment. His many studies "show that Australian cities adopting land value taxation only (LVT) experience a jump in building permits issued that far exceed the building permit increases of their like neighbors."[9]

Advantages Compared with Taxation

1. *The amount is determined by the market, not by government decree.* If one site brings twice the selling price of another, or twice the annual return, this is because the market judges it to be worth twice as much. And under the system proposed here, the same market activity would continue: the market would continue to assess the worth of land. But the greater part of the annual return would be taken by the government. This is in sharp contrast to taxation, which is fixed by government decree. Under the proposed reform, worth would replace will as the determinant.

A number of benefits would result. It would remove the uncertainty of not knowing what changes the authorities might choose to make: raising taxes, or lowering them, or changing from one kind of tax to another, or exempting some tax payers, or abolishing exemptions for others. In Britain in the 1970's, "tax rates on earnings rose steeply to 90 per cent and income from investments was taxed at an incredible 98 per cent."[10] A second benefit: at present pressure groups gain privileges by influencing the shape of the taxation system. Manufacturers may pressure the politicians into imposing import duties; or people without big families may influence the imposition of consumer taxes disadvantaging those families. But such bias is impossible with site revenue. A third benefit is that, in regard to site revenue, politicians could not choose to spend recklessly, since the amount received would be independent of their will. This is of particular relevance if it is a case of replacing all taxes with site revenue.

2. *The payment of site revenue to the government cannot be passed on.* By comparison, say a sales tax is imposed. It will be added to the price of the goods, so the consumer will be the ultimate payer. Similarly, an income tax rise will bring higher wages, and again the consumer pays. But the taking of the differential rent of sites cannot be shifted, because competition prevents it. Just as the market determines the amount to be paid, so it prevents the payment being passed on. Think of two sites, one renting for $50,000 a year, the other for $100,000. Suppose the owner of the more expensive land decided to pass on to the customers the additional payment over and above that of the cheaper land. So he raised his prices above those of his competitor with the $50,000 land. The result? He would price himself out of the market.

Or look at it in terms of supply and demand. When the government takes site revenue, the supply of land is not diminished nor is the demand increased. There is even, in a sense, an increased supply, for although the area remains the same, land will tend to be used more efficiently, since the owner has to pay the market assessment even if the land is underutilised. As for demand, users are willing to pay the same as previously, for the benefits are unchanged. It follows, as Samuelson and Nordhaus say, that "*the whole of the tax has been shifted backward onto the owners of the factor in inelastic supply.*

"Land owners will surely complain. But under perfect competition there is nothing they can do about it, since they cannot alter the total supply and the land must work for whatever it can get."[11]

Nearly all economists have agreed with the judgment of John Stuart Mill a century and a half ago: "A tax on rent falls wholly on the landlord. There are no means by which he can shift the burden upon anyone else."[12]

What is wrong with a tax that can be passed on? A number of things. Firstly, the alleged equity of a tax is destroyed. Suppose the tax on high incomes is increased, with the aim of distributing incomes more evenly. If the taxpayers pass it on, the government's aim is frustrated. The customers of a highly paid professional, including the poor customers, may end up paying the increase! Secondly, big families can suffer, as when each member needs an article - bread, shoes, and so on - and one wage earner has to earn the total passed on tax. Thirdly, if the tax is imposed at an early stage of production, the extra expense it entails will be passed down the line, together with the tax itself. A farmer will need extra capital to pay for a tractor with sales tax added to its price, and will want a return on the additional capital. This will mean higher costs for the other people in the production process, who in turn will raise their prices accordingly.

It is an intriguing fact that, whereas taxes increase the price of the thing taxed, site revenue decreases the price. Put a tax on wages, interest or goods, and they will rise in compensation. But when the government collects site revenue, the land falls in price. The reason is that the price is a capitalisation of the value of the advantages the land affords; and these are offset by the payment the owner has to make to the government. I will not be willing to give as much for a piece of land on which I have to pay a yearly amount to the government as on a piece without this expense.

3. *Site rent is almost impossible to evade.* Land cannot be hidden, while the fact that the market assesses the amount precludes the misrepresentations often possible with taxes. Sharp practices, the mania for finding tax loopholes, corruption: these are excluded.

The rich and powerful, who are so often in a better position to avoid taxes than the poor and uninfluential, are put on the same level as other citizens. Further, the state is saved the expense associated with preventing and detecting evasion. Moreover, there is none of the oppressive intrusion into our affairs which looms so large in the collection of taxes.

4. *Site revenue does not retard or distort production.* Although the government takes what would otherwise have gone to individuals, the pattern of production is not disturbed. To quote Samuelson and Nordhaus again: "A tax on pure economic rent will lead to no distortions or inefficiencies."[13] The reason is that the supply of land is not decreased and the demand for it remains unchanged; the difference being that now a portion of the rent, or a larger portion than before, becomes public revenue instead of passing into private hands.

Henry George brings out well the punitive effect of taxes on production. "If I have saved while you wasted, I am mulct, while you are exempt. If a man build a ship we make him pay for his temerity, as though he had done an injury to the state...We say we want capital, but if any one accumulate it, or bring it among us, we charge him for it as though we were giving him a privilege. We punish with a tax the man who covers barren fields with ripening grain, we fine him who puts up machinery, and him who drains a swamp."[14] Every tax on workers or investors tends to discourage production. The sentiment tends to be: "Why bother when I'm going to lose a big slice in taxes?"

Taxes also have a distorting effect, as areas of enterprise are sought upon which taxes fall less heavily - which are not necessarily the ones most needed.

Other Advantages

Having compared site revenue with taxation, let us look at benefits of this revenue apart from the comparison with taxation.

1. *It eliminates speculative rent.* To recall the meaning of speculative rent, it is a **return based on the expected future situational advantages**. If I buy land whose benefits are expected to grow, the expectation will be reflected in the price I must pay. Now, suppose the government is taking nearly all the annual site revenue. What prospect have I of gaining from the growth expected in future years? None; for when it comes the government will take more revenue, in accordance with the market assessment.

A fundamental fact is that, whereas speculation in products increases production, speculation in land decreases it. The reason: the high prices resulting from the former induce manufacturers to produce more, but the high prices from land speculation add to the manufacturers' costs, slowing production down. Remember that land is in fixed supply; we can't make more when it gets scarce. Also, consumers have less to spend when land speculation adds to the price of homes.

In boom periods land values rise, with speculators continually pushing them higher (and often borrowing recklessly to buy more land), until they reach unrealistic levels; and finally industry slows down - particularly the building industry, for people cannot afford the high land prices. Then comes recession. Land speculation is a basic cause of recessions.

2. *It encourages the best use of land.* With no site revenue payable to the government, owners at times either leave land unused or use it less effectively than they could, while waiting for it to become more valuable. As the previously quoted survey by the British Department of the Environment stated: "Because land without buildings is unrated, they [rates] do nothing to stimulate the re-use of vacant land."[15] Or I may be content to have my land as a car lot for a few years, until it is needed for a skyscraper. But with sizeable annual sums going to the state as site revenue, I will be eager to find the optimal use.

3. *It makes land cheap.* Land price falls as the percentage of government site revenue rises. With the system in full operation, land would sell for a small fraction of its present price.

One advantage is a mitigation of the urban sprawl which is a feature of modern society, a situation caused partly by unaffordable land prices. People are forced further out, where sites are cheaper. To take a striking example, Japanese workers have to endure long, wearying journeys from outlying districts into Tokyo because of the colossal price of more conveniently located land. Not only does this affect those directly involved; it adds to the cost of providing roads and all the services needed for a sprawling population as compared with a more compact condition.

Home ownership becomes far easier to achieve with cheap land, for the land is a large part, in some cases the larger part, of the total expense. Much smaller loans will suffice, if any loan is needed; and therefore an enormous sum will be saved in the interest payments that, currently, often run for twenty-five years or more, and far exceed the total cash payment for the house and land combined.

4. *It reduces privilege*. Recall that privilege is **a power accorded by the state to some, with undue discrimination against others**. It is verified in the present land system, not only through owners reaping benefits that should be common to all, but through the advantages owners enjoy over those unable to afford land.

Land owners' power and privilege has long been recognised. Adam Smith comments that the rent of land "...is not at all proportioned to what the landlord may have laid out upon the improvement of the land, or to what he can afford to take; but to what the farmer can afford to give."[16] Karl Marx spoke of "the monstrous power wielded by landed property, [which] when united hand in hand with industrial capital, enables it to be used against labourers engaged in their wage struggle as a means of practically expelling them from the earth as a dwelling place."[17]

E.G.Wakefield argued, in the nineteenth century, that land prices in the British colonies should be kept artificially high so that workers would not easily be able to own it, and would therefore be dependent on employers. Proceeds from land sales would be used to import sufficient workers to ensure that the supply always exceeded the demand. The practice in South Australia was based on Wakefield's plan, so that by 1899 forty-two families controlled two million acres.

Clyde Cameron, former Australian Minister for Labour, outlines the above facts and continues: "As land was developed, and the demand for labour increased, money from further land sales was used to bring in more of Britain's unemployed artisans and labourers in order to maintain a permanent pool of unemployed workers competing against each other to avoid starvation.

"The North American slaves had no such fear of starvation; and the convicts of South Australia's Sister Colonies were always assured of food regardless of whether work was organised for them. Freedom, the migrants soon discovered, meant no more than freedom to starve, or to work for slave rates of pay."[18]

Privilege is associated in various ways with our land system, as when rezoning, especially where it involves corruption, bestows windfall gains on a favoured few. But the fundamental bias is in the power of owners over non-owners, where the latter are discriminated against by high prices. It is a heavy bias in poor agricultural communities, but exists everywhere. Winston Churchill, an ardent advocate of public appropriation of site revenue, declared that land monopoly "is by far the greatest of monopolies - it is a perpetual monopoly, and it is the mother of all other forms of monopoly."[19]

References

[1] See *Costing the Earth*, edited by R.Banks, London, Shepheard-Walwyn, 1989, pp.149f.

[2] DoE 1988: 39.

[3] *Ibid.*, 40.

[4] Adam Smith, *The Wealth of Nations*, London, Dent, 1960 reprint, book V, chapter 2, part 1, p.325 (volume 2).

[5] *Ibid.*, p.326.

[6] Mark Blaug, *Economic Theory in Retrospect*, Cambridge University Press, 1985, p.87.

[7] Mason Gaffney, in *Land Value Taxation*, edited by Lindholm and Lynn, University of Wisconsin Press, 1982, p.151.

[8] Quoted by Steven Cord, *Catalyst!*, Indiana, Henry George Foundation of America, 1979, preface.

[9] *Ibid.*, p.88.

[10] George Gilder, *Wealth and Poverty*, New York, Basic Books, 1981, p.173.

[11] Samuelson and Nordhaus, *Economics*, New York, McGraw-Hill, 1995, p.244, original italics.

[12] J.S. Mill, *Principles of Political Economy*, book V, chapter 3, section 2.

[13] Samuelson and Nordhaus, *ibid*.

[14] Henry George, *Progress and Poverty*, New York, Robert Schalkenbach Foundation, 1987 reprint, book IX, chapter 1, p.434.

[15] DoE 1988:39.

[16] Adam Smith, *Wealth of Nations*, London, Dent, 1960 reprint, book I, chapter 2, p.131.

[17] Karl Marx, *Capital*, Moscow, Foreign Languages Publishing House, 1962, III, p.754.

[18] Clyde Cameron, *How Labor Lost Its Way*, Melbourne, The Henry George League, 1984, pp.7f.

[19] Winston Churchill, *Liberalism and the Social Problem*, London, Hodder and Stoughton, 1939, p.318.

13

Objections and Replies

Let us consider a number of arguments against the proposal to take site revenue for public needs.

Objection 1. Haven't we enough taxes without adding another?

Reply. We have too many; the aim should be to eliminate them, replacing them with site revenue as the source of public funds. It will take time, and supposes other radical changes; meanwhile the gradual introduction of this method of funding would be accompanied by the reduction or removal of taxes. Site revenue would replace them; it would not be added to them.

Nor is it a tax, although commonly called "the single tax". But strictly a tax is **the taking of private property for public purposes**, whereas this revenue belongs to the community. Of its essence it is public property, for society (and to a lesser degree the physical environment) is the cause of it.

Objection 2. State appropriation of ground rent implies state ownership of the land: for the one to whom rent is paid must be the owner. Under this proposed scheme the state becomes the landlord and those occupying the land become the tenants. Henry George, therefore, often insists that private property in land should be abolished. As a result he encountered strong opposition from people who considered private ownership of land to be a basic right. The contrast could hardly appear more clearly than it does in the fierce controversy that raged in the Catholic Church in the United States towards the end of the nineteenth century, when a priest, Dr Edward McGlynn of New York, was forbidden by his archbishop to teach George's doctrine that private property in land should be abolished. His refusal led to his excommunication.

Reply. Henry George certainly stated - numerous times - that private property in land must be abolished, making it common property. But the expression is rightly described by Robert V. Andelson as one of George's "terminological idiosyncrasies"; and he adds that the statement " 'We must make land common property' has hung from the beginning like a millstone around the neck of the movement he created, notwithstanding that even as he used the phrase he took pains to explain that by 'common property' he meant something very different from what it is ordinarily understood to mean."[1]

As George says: "We propose leaving land in the private possession of individuals, with full liberty on their part to give, sell, or bequeath it, simply to levy on it for public purposes a tax…"[2] One with the power of disposal here spoken of is the land's owner, not a tenant of the government. Confusion can come from failing to grasp the nature of ground rent, a failure made easier by the fact that the word rent has a different sense in everyday use, where it means payment to an owner. But so far as site revenue arising from social advantages is concerned, "land price" is no more the price of land than moonlight is the light of the moon: it is the price of access to the common good generated by society.

Had Father McGlynn been more careful with his terminology he might possibly have avoided the controversy in which he became embroiled. But he was eventually cleared. Pope Leo XIII appointed Archbishop Francisco Satolli to examine the case; McGlynn wrote a clear statement of his position, which was studied by Satolli and four professors of the Catholic University of America; and they rendered the unanimous judgment that there was nothing contrary to the Christian Faith or Catholic doctrine in the land philosophy preached by Dr McGlynn.[3]

Objection 3. It would be unjust not to pay compensation to landlords if this proposal were introduced; yet such payment would be impracticable, as the outlay would be so enormous that no government could afford it.

The community accepts that the selling price of land will not be almost taxed out of existence. People buy land with the confidence that they are not going to see the value nearly disappear with a change in government policy. Therefore the implementation of the new system would betray the land owning public. It would amount to robbing people of property the state had implicitly guaranteed.

Reply. The change would not be introduced overnight, taking everyone by surprise. We could expect a long period of debate to precede its acceptance, at least in a democracy, the necessary political support being gained only slowly. And with the likelihood of its acceptance, the speculative element in land prices would ease, for it would be feared that the expected increase would be taken by the state.

Most advocates of the reform support its gradual implementation, and rightly so. The percentage collected at first would be small, rising over a period of years. So the fall in prices need not be steep.

Then too, the land owners' benefits would at least partly offset their losses. In selling a property to move to another one, while the selling price would be down, so would the buying price of the new one. Again, the reform would replace any tax on improvements, leaving the owner free to build or make other improvements without incurring the penalty of taxation. More generally, since this revenue would replace taxes previously levied, losses would be balanced or reduced by taxation savings. In addition, the vast benefits flowing from the reform include the encouragement given to enterprise and to saving when these are free from the burden of taxation, and the lower interest rates when the taxation component is removed. Housing would be far cheaper, for the land would cost little. And the whole economy would run more smoothly, with a diminishing of the boom and bust conditions prevailing today.

The question comes down to whether the change would remove a great distortion, an unnatural anomaly, replacing it with a harmonious and natural distribution. If so, rejection of it for the reason under consideration amounts to rejecting an immense common good for the sake of limited and transient individual goods.

Objection 4. It is not true that the owner provides no service to the community. On the contrary, he is keen to put his land to the best use, for it will then sell for a higher price. So he performs the vital service of promoting the best use of land. Under the Georgist plan, however, he would not be rewarded for this, and therefore would lack the incentive. So instead of sites being more efficiently allocated, they would be allocated less efficiently. Briefly, the market would lack the incentive to undertake this entrepreneurial task.

Reply. The return to the government would be decided by the market on the basis of the value of sites in the locality. If a particular owner utilised his land more efficiently than his neighbours, he would reap the benefit. If, for instance, a locality needed an Asian food shop, land used for that purpose would be more efficiently used than if devoted to a less needed alternative. The owner would be rewarded for his initiative, whether through the annual return, if he retained the property, or through the sale of the site to someone who wanted it for that purpose. In the latter case the owner might have to convince the potential buyer that the site really was more valuable for the purpose envisaged than was reflected in the rent currently collected by the state. The same applies today: the efficient allocation of land is a process accomplished by buyers and sellers.

Objection 5. Why pick on the landlords so exclusively? Why not take other rents, such as the excess earnings, over and above what will keep them in their present occupation, of tennis champions, pop singers, top actors, and so on?

Reply. As mentioned earlier, these earnings are called rent by many economists, but are different in nature from rent in the classical sense. Taking rent as **the return from situational advantages**, a return generated principally by the community, it has been shown that the community is entitled to it. If indeed an argument were found to exist in the case of rent in the wider sense used in this objection, that would mean simply that this too should be collected by the state; but it would not affect the proposal I am defending. However, those other "rents" are not only small compared with site revenue, but do not have the same distorting effects on the economy. As Winston Churchill said, in answer to the claim that valuable paintings should be taxed: "Pictures do not get in anybody's way."[4]

Objection 6. The "user pays" principle should be applied. Government funds should be gathered not only from site revenue, but from the activities where people burden the community with costs. It is right that there be a tax on tobacco because of the health costs incurred by the community through tobacco-induced illnesses, and a tax on alcohol for the same reason.

Reply. A radical distinction exists between the revenue due to the state to pay its proper expenses, and compensation due from people for costs they have caused or are likely to cause. Site revenue is the natural fund for the former purpose. "User pays" is a good principle, but I would add the caution that alleged costs must be closely scrutinised; otherwise governments, in their zeal to get money and their bureaucratic urge to interfere in people's business, will misuse the principle.

Objection 7. The site revenue proposal would place too heavy a burden on some people. Businesses, especially small ones, might be unable to pay in bad times. Likewise farmers when crops fail. Regarding residential land, what of pensioners? It would be wrong to force them out of a home they had occupied most of their life. Insecurity and uncertainty would be inevitable if the "reform" were enacted.

Reply. Since site revenue is determined by the market, it fluctuates with economic conditions. In bad times less would be paid. Also, cheap land would mean less borrowing, and therefore less to service the loans.

In the case of residential land, it is true that hardship could arise through the fact that the land is non-productive. To recall what we said in chapter eleven, whereas a site used for production is the efficient cause of the revenue (it produces the revenue), a non-productive site is the revenue's final cause (the desirability of the site, for non-productive purposes, causes people to pay the revenue, but the land does not generate it for them). Against the possibility of hardship, however, is the fact that the change would bring far greater prosperity than we currently enjoy, so people would be in a better position to meet the expense, or to make provision to meet it after retirement. With land at a small fraction of its present cost, home owners would be free of the massive mortgage payments burdening millions today. Further, taxation would have been eliminated, or at least vastly reduced. Finally, relief could be given when genuinely needed. No arrangement will abolish all hardship. Sickness in particular will always make it impossible for some to manage.

Objection 8. The revenue could not be accurately assessed. Generally it is not a question of vacant land, but of sites with buildings and other improvements. Since the Georgist concept calls for the collection of ground rent while leaving improvements untouched, it remains impracticable unless the value of these can be distinguished. But this cannot be done. Suppose a farmer tried to assess the value of his buildings, irrigation works, planted trees, ploughed and fertilised fields, crops, etc., as compared with the site alone. He could not do so. How, then, can it be done by government bureaucrats? The result would be guesswork, with excessive assessments for some and deficient assessments for others. Abuses and corruption would abound.

Reply. Firstly, the market would make the assessment, not government bureaucrats. And the market is already doing it every day! Take the instance in the objection: suppose the farmer decides to sell. Potential buyers will promptly put a price on his farm compared with others having greater or less improvements.

Secondly, the intention is to leave a small part of the revenue with the owner. Land would thus retain a selling price, although small compared with today's prices. It would be a measure of the amount pertaining to the site, as distinct from that belonging to improvements. If land prices fell almost to zero, this would show the revenue passing to the government to be dangerously close to the maximum; while an increase in land prices would show that more should be going to the government. As at present, the selling price of land would provide the means of distinguishing between site values and improvements. Any estate agent can distinguish between the two; it is being done constantly.

Thirdly, revenue from sites alone, leaving improvements untaxed, is already a widespread practice; most local governments in Australia, for instance, do this, and some in the United States and other countries. The Georgist plan would mean increasing the percentage (and perhaps having it collected at state or federal level). Rather than being difficult to assess, land alone is relatively easy to assess. In *The Assessment of Land Value*,[5] detailed discussion by economists and assessors shows a majority holding that its accurate assessment is practicable, while that of buildings is less so.

Fourthly, most taxes really are at an arbitrary rate. Why have a minimum income tax of, say, 25 per cent, rather than 20 or 30 or something else? And likewise with other taxes. Anyone who objects to site revenue being collected by the government, and advocates alternatives, is advocating the arbitrary instead of what has a natural standard of measurement.

Objection 9. This source would not provide sufficient revenue. Colin Clark branded as "ridiculously false" the contention that "if adequate taxation were imposed upon land, no other taxation would be necessary."[6] But resort to other taxes would refute the Georgist idea of a natural harmony, whereby site revenue pays the expenses of government, and private property remains with its owners.

Reply. Estimates for the United States in earlier times, when government expenditure was low, indicate that it would then have been sufficient. Wilfred I. King calculated that nearly twice the required amount would have been available before the Civil War, and sufficient until 1915.[7] According to Steven Cord, it might have been enough until the 1930s.[8]

Even with the colossal government spending of today, land revenue would provide a far greater proportion than is usually conceded, as various studies show. The situation in Great Britain is carefully researched in *Costing the Earth*, edited by Ronald Banks. The authors complain about the difficulty of obtaining reliable data (for this aspect of economic study is surprisingly neglected - a fact to remember in regard to the unsubstantiated contention of Clark), but arrive at conclusions showing site revenue to be a very sizeable part of total income. "The uniform view that the rent of land is a relatively insignificant value has been associated with an equally startling absence of facts upon which to base the assessment," says Banks.[9] A conservative estimate gives land rent (actual or imputed) as 22.4 per cent of the national income in 1985, rising to 25.5 per cent in 1988.[10]

Figures for the United States, calculated by Steven Cord, making use of data from the US Bureau of the Census and the Federal Reserve Board, give land rent as 28 per cent of the national income in 1981.[11]

The land values used in calculating the above figures include a speculative value component - anticipated higher returns in the future push up land prices. Also, a small percentage of the revenue would remain with owners, under the proposed reform. Even so, a large fund for public use remains. But would there be enough to replace all taxes? At first glance there seems a big gap. However, other factors enter the picture.

Firstly, the reform's implementation will make a huge contribution to a healthy economy (the benefits examined in the previous chapter demonstrate this), with higher site revenue as a consequence. Experience shows that land prices and site revenue rise in a thriving economy and fall in a depressed economy. This is not just because of fluctuations in speculation, but because of the higher benefits to which a site gives access in good times, and the lower benefits in bad times.

Secondly, under a healthy system (I mean the natural system as a whole, as outlined in this work), the government budget would be vastly reduced. For one thing, those requirements would diminish which have expanded due to our unhealthy political and social conditions. Unemployment benefits are one example. Also, with the state confining itself to its proper sphere (a matter to be focussed on in chapters seventeen and eighteen), its expenses would drop dramatically. This involves a greater application of the "user pays" principle.

Given the above considerations, it is reasonable to expect sufficient return from site rent to pay the expenses of government, with no taxation whatever.

References
1 Robert V. Andelson, *Critics of Henry George*, edited by Andelson, New Jersey, Associated University Presses, 1979, p. 387.
2 Henry George, *The Condition of Labor*, p. 8, in *The Land Question and Related Writings*, New York, Robert Schalkenbach Foundation, 1982.
3 Stephen Bell, *Rebel, Priest and Prophet*, New York, Robert Schalkenbach Foundation, 1968 reprint, p. 232. McGlynn's statement is reproduced on pp. 226 - 231.
4 Winston Churchill, *The People's Rights*, New York, Taplinger Publishing Company, 1971 reprint, p. 118.
5 *The Assessment of Land Value*, edited by Daniel M. Holland, Madison, University of Wisconsin Press, 1970.

6 Colin Clark, *Taxmanship*, London, Institute of Economic Affairs, Hobart Paper 26, 1964, p. 41.
7 Wilfred I. King, *The Wealth and Income of the People of the United States*, New York, Macmillan, 1915, pp. 160-162.
8 Steven Cord, *Henry George: Dreamer or Realist?*, Philadelphia, University of Pennsylvania Press, 1965, p. 234.
9 *Costing the Earth*, edited by Ronald Banks, London, Shepheard-Walwyn, 1989, p. 38.
10 *Ibid.*, p. 40.
11 Steven Cord, *American Journal of Economics and Sociology*, vol. 44, no. 3, p. 279 (1985).

14

Comparison of Wages, Interest and Site Revenue

The Three Returns

Adam Smith comments: "The whole annual produce of the land and labour of every country...naturally divides itself, as has already been observed, into three parts: the rent of land, the wages of labour, and the profits of stock."[1] We have analysed this division, the profits of stock corresponding to what we have called interest or the return to investment.

We saw that the production of wealth consists in applying labour, usually with the aid of capital, to natural resources. It is exemplified all the way from the stone age producer with a flint knife to the most sophisticated technology. In society, unlike Robinson Crusoe on his island, it is a communal operation, with the immense benefits that flow from human association, benefits shared especially by those occupying the better sites. The basic elements, therefore, are land, labour and capital; but we should never forget how enormously these are enhanced by the benefits of association.

Nor should it be forgotten that the worker is the principal cause of wealth and services. Land provides the site and the materials, capital is the instrument. Both serve the worker. And since labour is **the exercise of human activity in production**, all who exercise this activity are, to that extent, workers. The term applies to everyone from the unskilled manual labourer to the president of a multinational corporation. It embraces not only employees but the self-employed. Actually, it is the market which employs everyone, whether directly or indirectly.

A return pertains to each of the three factors: wages to the worker, interest to capital, site revenue to land; and the nature of the factor shows to whom the return belongs. Surely it is obvious that the return pertaining to work belongs to the worker, and that pertaining to capital belongs to the investor of capital. Likewise with land: a return produced by the community, and attaching to land, belongs to the community. This follows from the nature of the return, as previously shown in detail.

The Question of Profit

Economists often propose a fourfold return, profit being the fourth constituent. However, there is really no justification for saying profit is on a par with the other three. It is defined as the return to the entrepreneur after allowing for the returns to land, labour and capital. But all entrepreneurial functions come under the headings of labour, capital investments and land dealings. The entrepreneur exercises productive activity in planning and organising, and in this regard is a worker. In so far as "profit" accrues from this source, it is a return to labour - it is wages. In so far as it accrues from capital investment, it is interest. When it comes from dealings in land, it is site revenue or the capitalisation of that revenue.

What about the exceptional profit sometimes made by entrepreneurs? Well, this may be compensation for a risky investment, which is a return to capital. Just as high interest is paid for other high-risk investments, the entrepreneur too will sometimes receive what looks like an excessive reward, but which is a reasonable compensation for risk. Also, the possible futility of his labour has to be taken into account. He may have worked long hours over a long period with little return and the danger of ultimate failure.

What if he is an entrepreneurial genius who, as a result, is able to make large profits consistently? In that case the profits are a form of wages - **recompense for labour expended in production**. They are caused by his outstanding work as an entrepreneur.

But suppose an abnormally high profit results from monopolistic power. Is this distinct from site revenue, wages and return to investment? No; it means that one or more of these is excessive because of monopoly. Soaring land prices bring abnormal profits. Or if products are sold above a competitive price, the labour and capital employed bring excessive profits.

Justice in Distribution

The distribution of wealth into site revenue, wages and return to investment, each corresponding to the appropriate factor of land, labour or capital, manifests balance and harmony; but also indicates justice in distribution: each should receive a due, or equitable, share. Does this happen in existing societies?

Obviously not in the case of site revenue, which is privately appropriated and thus distorts the whole system, leaving the state with no revenue of its own, and forcing it to take private assets for public purposes. Many malfunctions follow, as argued in the previous two chapters. It is as though a person had one leg two inches shorter than the other. This single malformation would lead to further problems, like back pain and headaches. Similarly, an economic malformation as fundamental as the misappropriation of the community's proper revenue cannot exist as an isolated fault, but must provoke further maladies.

Nor have existing societies the balance that should exist in the distribution of wages and interest. This fault is partly because of the misuse of site revenue, and more generally because of a lack of economic freedom. In chapter three, dealing with freedom and competition, we explained how freedom of opportunity will lead to equitable returns, and how the one great enemy of social freedom is privilege, in the sense of **a power accorded by the state to some, with undue discrimination against others**.

True freedom of opportunity for workers, investors and consumers will bring just distribution; and it will be accomplished especially by the elimination of privilege.

References
[1] Adam Smith, *The Wealth of Nations*, London, Dent, 1960 reprint, book 1, chapter 2, p. 230 (volume 2).

15

The Meaning of Value

The Basic Concept

Since the days of Adam Smith economists have argued about value, although the discussion has waned in recent decades.[1] The concept itself, and its distinction from usefulness or value in use, has been recognised from ancient times; but its precise meaning and its relation to use value are still debated.

Aristotle expressed the fundamental distinction, pointing out that our possessions have two uses. "Both belong to the thing as such, but not in the same manner, for one is the proper, the other the non-proper or secondary use of it. For example, a shoe is used for wear, and is used for exchange; both are uses of the shoe."[2] Shoes are specifically for protecting the feet, not for exchanging. Similarly, food is for nourishment, motor cars are for transport, knives are for cutting. Each thing has its own use or uses; each product is designed for a purpose, for the satisfaction of a specific desire. But all products can be exchanged.

Now, things may exchange for a greater or lesser quantity of other things. They have value, in the sense of purchasing power. It is this capacity which makes exchange possible, and which therefore makes economic society possible. So producers are busily employed in making all sorts of articles they don't want, but which they want to exchange for things they personally find useful. Everything in the economy has two uses or values: a proper use (as that of shoes in protecting the feet), and a general use consisting in the power of exchangeability. It is this power we wish to examine.

Through the first of its uses a thing ministers to a specific desire, such as a desire to protect the feet. Through the second of its uses it ministers to the common desire to save effort. In chapter two we studied this desire and the way it permeates all human activity, including economic activity. We want to achieve our goals with a minimum of effort, for effort is never sought for its own sake, but is avoided where possible. By specialising in doing things at which we are good, then exchanging, we save effort; and beyond this immediate aim we acquire more commodities, of better quality; and have leisure for non-economic pursuits.

When we have something for exchange we want it to have a high value; that is, we want it to be such that it will purchase a lot in return. Or looked at from a slightly different angle, we wish to save ourselves effort through exchanging valuable things we possess. Value, therefore, can be defined: **Command over human exertion**.

This understanding of value is developed by Henry George[3], but a more common definition is in terms of exchangeable quantities. In *The Penguin Dictionary of Economics*, Bannock, Baxter and Davis define value in exchange as: "The quantity of other commodities (or, more usually, money) a commodity can be swapped for."[4] But a problem here is that value and price seem to be the same thing. And indeed the same dictionary defines price as: "What must be given in exchange for something"; which does not really differ from their definition of value.

However, if value is seen as "command over human exertion", its relation to price becomes clear, for the latter is value seen relatively, or the value of one commodity measured by another. In other words, it is one thing to say what value is (to give the essence, the nature, of value); it is another to measure a commodity's value in relation to something else. The former definition says *what value is*, the second (that of price) says *how much value* one commodity has in relation to another. The second concept, price, is: **The measurement of relative command over human exertion**. An alternative definition: **The quantification of value**. We give the price when we say an ounce of gold is worth x ounces of silver; or, more often, if a comparison is made between a commodity and money, as in saying a pen is worth a hundred dollars.

Another criticism of defining value in terms of relative quantities is that it does not show its nature, but remains superficial. For the reality called value is linked to the saving of effort, and is not clearly understood unless this connection is seen. Moreover, when the different ways of commanding exertion are considered, the question of justice arises, for value can be due to exploitation. But that issue is obscured when value is viewed in purely quantitative terms.

Is value good? Certainly to the person possessing a valuable thing it is, for it affords command over goods and services - purchasing power; or from the standpoint of the saving of effort, it allows the owner of the valuable thing to save toil by commanding the toil of other people. But from the buyer's standpoint, a high value is bad. Sellers want their commodities to have a high value, buyers want their purchases to have as little value as possible.

Therefore wealth and value are not the same. Wealth, as discussed in chapter six, consists of products having the power to satisfy wants; and they may have this to a high degree without being valuable in the economic sense; that is, without being able to command a lot in exchange.

Value always signifies the presence of toil, of arduousness: I must labour, or use the result of someone else's labour, to buy a valuable thing; and I exercise command over the labour of others when I sell something valuable. But since toil is the opposite of the saving of effort, and the latter is naturally aimed at by the economy, it can equivalently be stated that the economy naturally aims at the destruction of value. Society wants more wealth with less value. The reduction of value, therefore, is a sign of a progressive economy. Take the computer industry: computers have become cheaper than they were, with increased power. Or look at products as a whole, compared with past ages: far more wealth is available for the same effort.

Economists sometimes assert that there cannot be a general increase or decrease in value, because value is relative - one thing rising in value as another declines: gold, for instance, in relation to silver. But the assertion refers to price. If, however, we see value as **command over human exertion**, clearly it will rise when greater obstacles to production exist, and fall when obstacles are removed. So a more efficient economy will reduce value, as will improved technology.

Two Theories

Various theories have been proposed to explain value, two of which we will consider now: the labour theory and the marginal utility theory.

The labour theory of value. This has many variations, but its central idea is that the amount a commodity will bring in exchange comes from the labour of producing it. The greater the labour, the greater the exchange value.

Adam Smith taught the theory, although with ambiguities. He writes: "It is natural that what is usually the produce of two days' or two hours' labour should be worth double what is usually the produce of one day's or one hour's labour."[5] Karl Marx, who made his version of the theory the cornerstone of his economics, says that what "determines the magnitude of the value of any article is the socially necessary labour it contains, or the social labour time requisite for its production."[6]

One criticism of the theory is that when a new method of production is found which reduces the labour needed, the stock already produced by the old method will tend to fall in value; so the value will not correspond to the labour. Proponents of the theory can reply that it is today's labour costs, not those of a manufacturer whose equipment is out of date, that determine value.

Again, it is objected that fluctuations in the value of products occur independently of labour costs. If an article goes out of fashion, for instance, its value drops. Or if particularly good (or bad) seasons occur, with better (or worse) crops, the price swing is unrelated to the labour expended. The theory's defender may reply that fluctuations will even out in the long run, due to competition, and it is to the long run that the theory applies, not to each individual case in isolation.

Another objection is that not everything having value is the result of labour. Natural resources have value; licences have value - as in the right to a milk run in a zoned area, or the right to manufacture a machine under patent. Labour, therefore, cannot be the explanation, or at least not the sole explanation, of value.

The marginal utility theory. This widely accepted theory was first proposed in the nineteenth century, its main tenets being developed by Karl Menger, W.S. Jevons and Leon Walras. Also called the Austrian theory, it explains economic value through the interaction of desire and scarcity. Anything with value in the market must have a utility desired by buyers. Unless we see a commodity as in some way useful for satisfying a desire, we are not willing to buy it. But utility alone is insufficient, for some things have great utility and are desired, yet have no economic value. They are obtained free. Sunshine and fresh air are examples.

However, if the supply of a commodity is insufficient to satisfy desire for it, value arises. And the scarcer the commodity, the greater the desire. We ordinarily feel no strong desire for water, because we can get all we want just by turning the tap on. But if we were in the desert and in danger of being deprived of water, our desire would sharpen, even before any shortage occurred. Jevons says: "We may state as a general law that *the degree of utility varies with the quantity of commodity, and ultimately decreases as that quantity increases.*"[7]

Suppose I am very thirsty and would pay five times the usual price for a cup of coffee. After drinking one cup the situation will change: I may be willing to pay only twice the usual price for a second cup. Perhaps I would agree to a third cup at the usual price. But I would reject a fourth cup even if it were free, my desire for coffee having ceased.

The marginal utility theory maintains that the market price of a commodity is fixed by marginal buyers; that is, by those barely willing to buy at a certain price. If it were any higher they would not buy. If it went any lower a new margin would be set: a point where people who considered the previous price too high would now become buyers. But clearly there cannot be a range of prices according to the degree of desire experienced by each individual. The price at which a commodity is sold, and which is the highest certain buyers (the marginal buyers) will pay, must be less than some people would be willing to pay.

The marginal utility theory has had the effect of focussing attention on marginal changes and providing a method of analysing them. Consumer preference, for instance, is analysed in terms of the consumer's psychology. Indifference curve analysis takes commodities and asks whether the consumer prefers A or B, or is indifferent. Thus indifference curves are constructed. Likewise, the profit-maximising tendency of entrepreneurs or the most satisfying combination of work and leisure for employees can be studied and graphically represented.

The widespread favour enjoyed by the theory is partly because of its practical applications in the empirical investigations of economists. But the deeper question remains: Is this explanation of value correct?

An objection is that it fails to explain variations of value which occur when the cost of production rises or falls. If, for instance, a new invention reduces the cost of producing an article, the price tends to fall. When the contrary happens - an article becomes more expensive to produce - the price tends to rise. There is certainly a relation of cause and effect here: the cost of production causes a change in the price. While this does not show the cost of production to be the sole cause of value (and indeed it is not), it does show it to be one cause. It is true, as holders of the theory point out, that the change in price will involve adjustment to a lower or higher level of wants. But the change in the level of wants is caused by the change in costs.

The fact is that, while the marginal utility theory gives a worthwhile account of the psychological forces in the value situation, it fails to reach the underlying causes of value. I will argue that value has two sources, and that these must be understood if the meaning of value and its importance in economics are to be fully appreciated.

The Two Sources
Henry George distinguishes between value from production and value from obligation, discussing the matter at length in book II of *The Science of Political*

Economy. These two concepts allow us to classify the value found in things, and provide the means of judging what healthy value is.

Value from production. My definition is: **Command over human exertion, competitively determined, and arising from the expenditure of labour and capital**.

The first words - *Command over human exertion* - give the definition of value, from whichever source it comes. *Competitively determined*: this is the genuine competition we have contrasted with spurious competition. Workers, investors and consumers want to achieve their purpose with economy of effort; and under truly competitive conditions this is done without exploitation. So the command over exertion which *arises from the expenditure of labour and capital* and goes into the price of the product, constitutes its value (or that part of its value which is from production).

A couple of points need clarification. Firstly, it is not a question of the individual effort expended by this or that worker. One will find the same work more tiring or boring or unpleasant than another does; but the market ignores this. The remuneration is fixed socially, being the amount needed to call forth the required supply of labour. Secondly, a long run view has to be taken, for in the short term there will be fluctuations (such as particularly good or bad seasons, or unexpected surges or down turns in demand) which will eventually even out.

Briefly, value from production arises from the payment to workers and investors under conditions of true competition. Low payments mean low value in the article produced; high payments mean high value. If the payments could be magically removed, goods and services would have no value, but would be free - except for possible value from the source still to be examined.

"Haven't you overlooked some expenses?" I may be asked. "What about raw materials, electricity, depreciation, insurance of workers and of capital equipment? These add to the value of goods and services, and arise from 'the expenditure of labour and capital', to quote from your definition of value from production."

Regarding raw materials, electricity and similar items, the labour and capital needed for their production is the reason they have value (again leaving aside the source of value to be examined next). As for insurance of workers, this is part of the reward for labour, just as are other amenities offered to workers in addition to their pay packet. Capital equipment is insured because of its cost arising from payments to workers and investors.

Value without production. The second source of value is distinguished by the fact that it is unearned. It is: **Command over human exertion, arising**

from unearned advantages. Although found in a variety of things, it always has this characteristic: competitive labour and capital did not cause it. Instead, its source is in some other power, some advantage. Let us take examples, without trying to cover everything.

Money. Modern money, unlike the precious metals commonly used in earlier times, does not have value from production. The goods I buy with a hundred dollar note have no relation to the cost incurred by the government in manufacturing the note. The value is from agreement, and from legislation, to use those pieces of paper as a medium of exchange. Without that agreement and legislation my note would be worthless. But by the unearned advantage conferred by agreement and law, it has the power of commanding exertion by exchanging for goods and services: it has value.

Patents and copyright. The holder of these valuable rights can thereby command the exertion of other people through the price received for an invention or literary work. And the right is conferred by law, which gives it the character of an unearned advantage. Nevertheless, the product covered by the right is the result of work and capital, for which the inventor or writer is entitled in equity to a return. But he could well be robbed if patent or copyright laws did not exist. By the nature of the situation inventions and literary works would be open to appropriation by people who had done nothing towards their production. These laws, therefore, safeguard the right to value from the expenditure of labour and capital. So they are justified in principle, although care needs to be taken that the laws actually in place do not confer undue advantages.

Old masters. It is not production cost that gives the owner of the paintings the power of demanding a high price, and thereby commanding the labour of other people. The unearned advantage is the ownership of an article which is unique and desired.

A stock exchange seat. A milk run in a zoned area. The value of these privileges shows clearly in their selling price. It is not a value from production, but from an exclusive right which constitutes an unearned advantage.

Exploitation of workers. Exploitation by workers. Suppose an entrepreneur who appears to be getting value from production, but in reality exploits his workers, and whose return is in part due to that factor. Competitive conditions are absent, allowing him to make more than he would under conditions of freedom. He has a **command over human exertion arising from unearned advantages**. In its extreme form the power to force other human beings to work for one is found in slavery, where a human being can be bought or sold, the slave's value showing in the price. Or take a situation where artificial barriers to entry into a trade or profession exist, resulting in the power to overcharge because of the scarcity. To the extent that fees are above the competitive level there is value from unearned advantages.

Private appropriation of site revenue. Our discussion in earlier chapters established the unearned character of site revenue in private hands. It is the most fundamental case of value without production, for it pertains to one of the three original factors of production and it enables the land owner to derive a value from human association which should instead be applied to the needs of the community.

Marx's Surplus Value

Karl Marx says: "The values of commodities are directly as the times of labour employed in their production...The value of gold or silver, like that of all other commodities, is regulated by the quantity of labour necessary for getting them."[8] Our examination of the two sources of value shows that no labour theory is sufficient. Nevertheless, what we have said about value without production (or value from obligation, in George's terminology) has a direct bearing on Marx's concept of surplus-value.

Suppose, Marx says, that a man works for twelve hours. And suppose six hours is sufficient to (a) pay for the material he works up, the wear and tear on the machinery, etc.; (b) pay his wages. This means, in effect, that he is working six hours for nothing. He is creating value during that six hours, but it goes to the capitalist and the land owner. This is surplus-value; which is value created by the worker, but taken from him by the exploitative capitalist class. Marx sees it as determined by the labour that went into it.[9]

We are not concerned here with a detailed analysis of the theory, but with determining its relation to the value without production (or value from obligation) we are discussing.

One element Marx includes in surplus-value is the return received by the investor, which he claims is unjustifiable. But we concluded, in chapter nine, that there is justification for interest; and in accordance with that position we have, in the present chapter, classed interest, when competitively determined, as one of the elements giving rise to value from production. But it is true that under anti-competitive conditions an excessive, and exploitative, return can occur.

Marx states: "Rent, interest and industrial profit are only three different names for different parts of the surplus-value of the commodity, or the unpaid labour enclosed in it, and they are equally derived from this source, and from this source alone."[10] I have just commented on interest, a comment which also applies to industrial profit, if we want to put it in a category distinct from interest. Regarding rent: its private appropriation, as we have argued at length, is unjustifiable and constitutes unwarranted value without production. Marx is right in saying exploitation occurs here.

His concept of surplus-value identifies real areas of exploitation, although he wrongly includes all interest. It is a concept covered by the wider notion of value without production.

Value from Privilege

Value without production is not always a bad thing, as is especially obvious with money. But it is often bad - usually because, in those cases, the value is derived from privilege; namely: **A power accorded by the state to some, with undue discrimination against others**. This applies to certain instances of value given in the present chapter. A stock exchange seat or a milk run in a zoned area owe their value to discriminatory powers exercised or permitted by the state, which enable some to benefit through restrictions on the freedom of others. The same applies to most of the exploitation of workers and exploitation by workers, for the power over others which makes these practices possible is usually either supported by law (as in so many anti-competitive practices) or at least permitted (as with the intimidation exercised by some trade unions).

But the most far-reaching case of privilege giving rise to value is in the private appropriation of site revenue.

The menace of value from privilege appears more clearly when we realise its relative permanence compared with wealth, and its tendency to increase as contrasted with the tendency of value from production to decrease.

First, its relative permanence: think of a site with a factory standing on it. The factory will have an exceedingly brief life compared with the site, and will need constant maintenance to keep it from deteriorating. Most forms of wealth are similar: they deteriorate fairly quickly, and need labour expended on them to slow the process. How much of today's wealth existed a hundred years ago? Not much; and most of our current wealth will vanish within a century. Value from privilege, however, tends to be permanent. If the state allows me the revenue from that factory site, I can appropriate it for the rest of my life, then bequeath it to my heirs. Sites in London have provided revenue for centuries, and may continue to do so into the distant future. Other forms of value from privilege have the same property of relative permanence, such as licences capable of perpetuation from generation to generation.

Secondly, whereas value from production tends to fall, value from privilege tends to rise. New inventions, new skills, population growth: all effect a reduction in the effort of producing goods, and therefore a reduction in their value. Compare motor vehicle prices with those of eighty years ago. But what of a franchise or a piece of real estate? The same causes that reduce the value of products operate to raise the value of these things, for the owners, by means of their privilege, gain a share of the increased wealth.

References

1 See Donald Rutherford, *Dictionary of Economics*, London, Routledge, 1992, entry **Value**.
2 Aristotle, *Politics*, book I, chapter 9, 1257a, 7-9.
3 See his *The Science of Political Economy*, New York, Robert Schalkenbach Foundation, 1981 reprint, book II, chapter 13.
4 Bannock, Baxter and Davis, *The Penguin Dictionary of Economics*, London, Penguin, 1987.
5 Smith, *The Wealth of Nations*, London, Dent, 1960 reprint, book I, chapter 6, p. 42.
6 Karl Marx, *Capital*, translated by Eden and Cedar Paul, London, Dent, 1930, book I, chapter 1, p. 8.
7 W.S. Jevons, *The Theory of Political Economy*, London, Macmillan, 1888, 3rd edition, p. 53, original italics.
8 Marx, "Wages, Price and Profit", in *Selected Works* of Marx and Engels, New York, International Publishers, 1968, p. 207.
9 *Ibid.*, p. 214.
10 *Ibid.*, p. 215.

16
Money

The Great Medium of Exchange

Without money, economic life would be crippled. If the articles we manufactured and the services we rendered had to be paid for by an exchange of other articles or services, it would often be impossible to reach any satisfactory arrangement. A butcher, having only meat to exchange, would have to find someone willing to accept it in exchange for shoes or furniture or his other requirements. Roundabout exchanges rather than direct ones could often be made, but these, when possible, would be inconvenient.

Credit would alleviate the problem, but would leave many debts outstanding for long periods, awaiting the opportunity for suitable exchanges.

Measuring the value of articles would present a further difficulty. The butcher and his customers would be faced with making an assessment of a leg of lamb's value relatively to a pair of shoes, a kitchen table, tuition for the butcher's child, or a bus fare. The difficulty would increase when payment was deferred, as the value of the articles decided upon would fluctuate between the commencement of the deal and its conclusion - perhaps in a year's time.

There is also the question of saving. In what form would goods be held for future exchange? Things fluctuate in value, many cannot be stored without rapid deterioration, many take up a lot of space.

Money has the purpose of overcoming these difficulties. Essentially it is a medium of exchange; and consequently it functions as a measure of value and as a store of value. What is an economic exchange? It is the giving of products or services and the receiving of other products or services instead. But when money is given in payment, only half an exchange has been made. Instead of my wheat being swapped for your butter, you give me money for the wheat. Only half an exchange of products has occurred. The exchange will not be completed until I use the money to buy something. And here is the principal reason for money: it breaks an exchange into two parts. This solves the difficulty which would otherwise have prevented the existence of a complex system with a minute division of labour: the difficulty of each party to a potential exchange having nothing the other wanted. Because money can be swapped for all other things, it is the best measure of value. Rather than trying to compare a variety of products with each other, we compare them all with what they most readily exchange for - money. I don't evaluate a pound of meat in terms of a quantity of potatoes, but in terms of a sum of money.

Money is also a convenient store of value: it is easy to keep on hand for future purchases, rather than amassing a quantity of furniture or other saleable articles.

Definition of money. As with other terms, its use varies between economists. In their *Dictionary of Economics*, Sloan and Zurcher exclude cheques from the notion of money, but include them under currency, which they use in a wider sense than money.[1] But they note (in the entry **money**) that some authorities reverse the order, using currency in the more restricted sense. Bannock, Baxter and Davis, in *The Penguin Dictionary of Economics*,[2] are among those who have this reverse order. Some uses of the word money include forms of credit, which obscures the nature of credit.

As understood here, money is: **A generally acceptable medium of exchange which finalises a transaction**.

Medium of exchange. Here is the key point. Money stands as the medium in an exchange, not a terminus. When wheat is exchanged for money, and later the money for butter, the two extremes or termini are wheat and butter, no matter how long the time between the two transactions. The money is not a terminus, but a medium, serving to facilitate an exchange of products.

Generally acceptable. A thing is not money if it functions in a very limited way as a medium in exchanges, as it lacks that comprehensive power of facilitating buying and selling throughout the economy which is the very purpose of money. When I accept money in payment, it is because I am confident of easily disposing of it in buying what I want. This is one reason for not classing a cheque as money; but there is another reason which we will look at now.

Finalises a transaction. When we give money in return for a product or a service, the transaction is finished. And in this respect money differs from credit, which can be defined: **Purchasing power obtained by means of a promise to pay**. Strictly speaking, a cheque is credit, for when I offer a cheque I am in effect promising that payment will be made by the bank. But it may not be; the cheque may bounce.

Although the line between money and credit is frequently blurred in economic discussion, the two should be distinguished, for there is a clear-cut difference between payment and a promise to pay. The distinction is also important in dealing with questions of instability and inflation, where excessive credit is a major culprit.

Money As a Terminus of Exchange

In dealing with money as a medium, we have been looking at it formally - that is, precisely as money. But there are ways in which it is a terminus of exchange, not a medium. And to consider it in this respect is to view it materially - as a reality, but not in its function as a facilitator of exchange.

Take commodity money, as contrasted with token money. Historically, many things have been used as a medium of exchange which also functioned regularly as articles of commerce apart from their role in facilitating exchanges. Gold, silver, grain, rum and many other commodities have performed both functions. In Germany after the Second World War cigarettes were used as money because their value was more stable than that of the official currency. When their value fell, more were smoked, which raised the value again! Token money, by contrast, is manufactured to be used as money, and its value is not derived from any prior value as a commodity.

Another way in which money functions as a terminus of exchange, not a medium, and therefore is not formally money, is in the buying and selling of rare coins. If a dealer sells a coin for £100, the coin is a terminus of the exchange, while the £100 is the medium. The coin is the thing the buyer wants, not a medium through which something else is obtainable.

Likewise, in the international money market, if so many yen are exchanged for so many American dollars, the two currencies are the termini of the exchange. They are the commodities wanted by the exchanging parties, not a medium through which commodities are exchanged. And because money is here being bought and sold as a commodity (it is not functioning precisely as money), its price fluctuates according to market conditions.

This fact provides the answer to the fear that free trade will lower our wages by subjecting our workers to competition from poorly paid workers overseas. It is true that cheap imports will mean less jobs in the affected categories, but there will be more in other categories, for an increase in imports requires an increase in exports. If imports become excessive compared with exports, the value of our currency will fall, for less demand will exist for it. After all, why would other countries want our currency except for buying things from us, directly or indirectly? So "cheap imports", in the absence of exports will become dear imports, because more of our money will be needed to pay for them.

In the buying and selling of currencies, as in the buying and selling of other things, there should be a free market, for the currencies function as so many commodities (not as media of exchange). Milton and Rose Friedman point out "...there can be no balance of payments problem so long as the price of the dollar in terms of the yen or the mark or the franc is determined in a free market by voluntary transactions."[3] A corollary: government intervention to control the exchange rate is an interference with the free market, just as when other prices are controlled. [4]

True and Spurious Money

Suppose a counterfeiter uses his fake bank notes to buy goods. How is his action different from the use of legitimate notes?

The forger has obtained goods without producing corresponding goods (or equivalent services). The "money" he manufactures has no backing in goods or services. Therefore it is not really a medium in his transactions. For the character of money as a medium is that it stands between two commodities: it splits into two what would otherwise be a bartering of goods. But if there are no goods (or services) backing the "money" (that is, no goods for which the alleged money was earned), then it cannot be a medium. Instead it is a terminus. It stands at one end of the transaction. It is pathological, a perversion of true money, and enables its originator to live at the expense of people who earn their return by working or investing.

Ordinarily counterfeiting activity is too small to have any significant economic effect. But its tendency is to produce inflation, for the pseudo-currency dilutes the money supply. In effect, there is too much money, so its value drops, making things more expensive. If counterfeiters could keep extending their operations, the eventual result would be extreme inflation. But governments do essentially the same thing! It is called "printing money", and this has literally been done, as with the French assignats in 1789. Usually, however, it is less blatant.

In the United States the Treasury can sell bonds to the Federal Reserve System, which pays for them either by printing bank notes or by a book entry showing a credit to the Treasury which is then drawn on to pay bills.[5] In either case money is created out of thin air, for it has no backing in goods and services, but is equivalent to the counterfeiter's operation. It is not a medium of exchange, but stands at one end, replacing the products and services that should be there.

This is spurious money, for it contradicts the very nature of money, which is a medium. It can be defined: **A terminus of exchange masquerading as a medium**. It is essentially inflationary, diluting the money supply just as truly, though less obviously, as did the rulers of former times who mixed base metals with silver in their coinage.

Inflation

Inflation is sometimes viewed as a persistent increase in the price level, sometimes as a decline in the value of money. The latter emphasis is better, as indicating the insidious dilution of which we have been speaking. Inflation is: **A fall in the value of money**. However, this does not deny that non-monetary factors can contribute.

There is cost-push inflation, where production costs send prices up. This happens, for instance, when a wage rise leads to flow-on rises for other workers. It happened dramatically after oil prices quadrupled in 1973. There is also demand-pull inflation, when the demand for goods and services exceeds the supply, enabling sellers to charge higher prices. Although monetarists argue that cost-push and demand-pull factors do not have a continuing effect on price levels, their view does not make sufficient allowance for the extent to which price spirals are built into modern economies. When wages rise, the price of goods increases, which leads to further wage rises. The cycle is hard to break.

But beneath these causes, and aggravating them, is the dilution of the money supply. A vivid historical example is found in the case of Virginia and its neighbouring colonies during and after the seventeenth century. The basic money, and at times the only legal currency, was tobacco. But because the cost of growing it was less than the original price set on it in English currency, it was produced in large quantities. The result was inflation, due directly to money (tobacco) falling in value compared with other things. After half a century of inflation, prices relatively to tobacco had risen forty-fold.

Another example of the same phenomenon is found in the use of silver and gold as money. Inflation occurred in Europe when these metals flooded in from Mexico and South America. Likewise, inflation occurred in the nineteenth century due to the gold discoveries in California and Australia.

Putting the question, "Does the quantity of money grow rapidly because prices increase rapidly, or vice versa?", Milton and Rose Friedman argue, in accordance with their monetarism, that the causative agent is the growth in the money supply.[6] They offer as an indication the fact that "on most of the charts the number plotted for the quantity of money is for a year ending six months *earlier* than the year to which the matching price index corresponds." They argue also that evidence is provided from an examination of the institutional arrangements that determine the quantity of money. Again, there are "a large number of historical episodes in which it is crystal clear which is cause and which is effect." The American Civil War provides a striking example. The South printed money to help finance the war, and inflation averaged ten per cent a month for a two and a half year period to March 1864. But when a monetary reform was enacted, the price level quickly dropped.

From our analysis of spurious money, which is a terminus of exchange masquerading as a medium, it follows that when governments create this "money" they are doing something which is inflationary of its very nature. It is this which monetarism rightly condemns.

Easy credit, too, plays a big part in causing inflation. We have defined credit as: **Purchasing power obtained by means of a promise to pay**; and from the definition we see how credit can provoke inflation. It allows people to spend before they have produced the goods and services needed to pay for the spending. When this happens on a large scale, demand will tend to outstrip supply: goods will be wanted before sufficient have been produced, which leads to demand-pull inflation. In this case, as in that of spurious money, there is an excessive increase in the money supply.

Who is to blame for inflation? If politicians are to be believed, the culprits include greedy business men, trade unions, the weather, foreign countries, and various other disturbing influences. However, if we look at the facts, it becomes clear that the government is largely to blame. This is obvious in regard to spurious money. As for excessive credit, government manipulation is often responsible, attempting to stimulate the economy in this way.

While cost-push factors are complicated, the persistent price spirals would hardly be possible without the rigidities caused by government policies. These may take the form of inaction, as when militant unions are allowed to get away with tactics against employers which would bring court charges if practised by ordinary citizens. Or when they are allowed to intimidate their own members. Or when closed shop policies are permitted. On the other hand, legislation to preserve wage relativities contributes directly to the spiral.

Land speculation, due to the state not taking its proper revenue, is another contributor to rising prices. With a booming economy, land prices in particular rise sharply, for speculation pushes them up, and the remedy when products rise in price - greater production - is not available here, for the quantity of land is inelastic.

If government interference were removed, the granting of privileges to favoured groups ceased, and true competition reigned, inflation would vanish. For it is like a high fever, signifying an abnormality, a disease. With affairs running normally, nothing would exist to cause a persistent fall in the value of money. Even an exceptional event like the oil price jump of the 1970s would not have the flow-on effects that are built into our present system. At any time some prices are rising and others are falling, but no factor pertaining to a healthy economy would cause a persistent general rise.

Inflation is a serious disease. John Maynard Keynes wrote after the First World War: "There is no subtler, no surer means of overthrowing the existing basis of society than to debauch the currency. The process engages all the hidden forces of economic law on the side of destruction, and does it in a manner which not one man in a million is able to diagnose."[7]

Even relatively minor inflation has serious effects. It robs those whose savings do not rise accordingly, as in long term investments. It discourages saving, for people tend to buy now rather than save if they expect price rises to outstrip their savings. It disrupts economic life by sending the wrong signals, as we saw in chapter five when dealing with the reality which constitutes the central nervous system of the economy, namely the price system. Inflation is disruptive also in causing high interest rates, which make investment more difficult and impose a frightening burden on people struggling to pay off their homes.

The whole area of monetary control is one where the state interferes with the free working of the economy. When the reserve bank forces interest rates up or down in pursuance of a plan to slow things down or speed them up, this is a direct interference with the market. It is profoundly serious because of its immense repercussions throughout society. It is like a doctor prescribing drugs, perhaps with drastic side effects, to counter an illness. The ideal is to eliminate the cause of the illness, so that the body can function naturally and protect itself without the aid of dangerous foreign substances.

Similarly with the economy. Working naturally, it will not need the violence of state intervention. Should intervention, as in the manipulation of interest rates, be needed, it is because of radical maladies in the economic system. They should be identified and eliminated, allowing the economy to function naturally. Government manipulation of the money supply is at best a temporary measure constituting the lesser of two evils. Whereas the doctor may not ever be able to dispense with drugs for a particular patient, due to chronic deterioration, the economy can attain health, as this book is endeavouring to make clear.

References

[1] Sloan and Zurcher, *Dictionary of Economics*, New York, Barnes and Noble, 1961.
[2] Bannoch, Baxter and Davis, *The Penguin Dictionary of Economics*, London, Penguin, 4th edition, 1987.
[3] M. and R. Friedman, *Free to Choose*, Melbourne, Macmillan, 1980, p. 44.
[4] On balance of trade implications for an economy, see Walther Lederer, "Balance of International Trade", in *The McGraw-Hill Encyclopedia of Economics*, editor in chief D. Greenwald, New York, McGraw-Hill, 1994.
[5] M. and R. Friedman, *ibid.*, p. 265.
[6] *Ibid.*, pp. 256ff.
[7] J.M. Keynes, *The Economic Consequences of the Peace*, New York, Harcourt, Brace and Howe, 1920, p. 236.

17

The Place of the Government

Murray Rothbard claims that "*every* service can be supplied on the free market", including police and military protection, and judicial protection.[1] At the opposite extreme from this radical individualism stands the discredited system of Marxism, with its endeavour to bring every important area of life under state control. The government's true place can be established from considerations already discussed, which is what we must do now, leaving till the following chapter an examination of state encroachments on personal freedom.

Civil Authority
Each of us is a person and a part. This distinction, dealt with in chapter one, forms the basis for an understanding of the extent of true state authority. As we saw, each person has inalienable rights, including the right to freedom. Each is a being possessing an intellect and will, and with potentialities surpassing the boundaries of any political or social system. So we owe only a limited subjection to any system. On the other hand, each of us is part of a social whole; and a part, precisely as such, is for the sake of the whole - as the hand serves the whole body. I owe service and allegiance to the society of which I am a part.

As observed in chapter one, the family and civil society are required by human nature, and in that sense are natural societies. But what of government? Could it be dispensed with?

A philosophical principle states, "There is no coordination without subordination", and this provides the answer. Even a sport requires officials with authority, as does any business firm. Otherwise the activities of the individuals in the group lack coordination and become chaotic. But if authority is necessary in small groups, it will be far more imperative in civil society, containing millions of people and addressing a vast range of issues.

However, the state should do no more than necessary, in accordance with the principle of subsidiarity: **What can be done by an individual or smaller group should not be assigned to a larger group**. So it comes to this: are there functions which are needed and which the state alone is able to do satisfactorily? The area of competence will comprise those things required for the civil community's defence and the promotion of its welfare, in so far as others lack the prerogative, or lack the initiative, or default from their duty. Let us take these in turn.

The government's duties. There are things for which others lack the prerogative. Included here are all the laws imposed on the society. I may think certain traffic regulations would be a good idea - perhaps a reduction in the speed limit or the provision of more one-way streets - but I have no authority to impose my view. Nor has any particular group in the community. The same applies to any law. Should some diseases be notifiable? What regulations should be made concerning marriage and divorce? Should prostitution or pornography be illegal? If laws are to be enacted, a legitimate authority must enact them, which can only be a government authority, whether at local, state or federal level as appropriate. Were individuals or particular groups to take this function on themselves, the result would tend to tyranny; nor could they justify imposing their will on people who disagreed.

Secondly, some things should be done by the government because others lack the initiative. The provision of public roads is an example. In certain circumstances privately constructed roads with a toll to pay the cost would be feasible, but this is usually impracticable, owing to the vast number of roads and streets. However, the government's part should be kept to the necessary minimum. No justification exists for the construction workers being government employees. The government's task in road building is to make the final decision about what is needed, to oversee the project and to pay the cost.

Thirdly, the government must step in when others default from their duty and there is no effective alternative to government intervention. An instance is the matter of safety regulations. Say firms are neglecting the safety of their employees or the public. The government is entitled - may have a duty - to prescribe reasonable standards and ensure their enforcement. Again, when society is malfunctioning because of neglect of the natural laws that should be promoted, the state will need to intervene in ways which would otherwise be unnecessary. The state may have a duty to provide pensions because people have been unable to save for their retirement.

Government action on pollution and other forms of environmental damage can be justified, in some circumstances, on all three grounds: others may lack the prerogative and the initiative to take effective action, and also default from what they can and should do.

We mentioned that Murray Rothbard advocates the provision of all services by the free market, eliminating the government. He argues that even the provision of military and police services should be by free enterprise. "Defense services, like all other services, should be marketable and marketable only."[2] He claims: "No state or similar agency is needed to define or allocate property rights." He thinks a system of freely competitive police and military services should be inaugurated, with the services most probably sold "on an advance subscription basis, with premiums paid regularly and services to be supplied on call."[3] Judicial services, too, would be freely competitive.

Surely the fatal weakness in his proposals is that defence and judicial services, from their nature, cannot be supplied on market principles. An agreed code of laws is necessary, but there is no market process whereby the code could be acquired. While the basic principles are inherent in man and society, they have to become known and accepted for a legal system to be workable; and the operations of the market will not achieve this. Then there are the numerous positive laws (not opposed to natural principles, but not prescribed by them either) which society has to legislate. A market process is not competent to produce them. Rothbard speaks of the limitation of appeals under a free market system, and says: "*Every* legal system needs some sort of socially-agreed upon cutoff point, a point at which judicial procedure stops and punishment against the convicted criminal begins."[4] He does not explain how decisions of this kind could be reached by a market process.

Many people in any society will either not see what should be done, or not want to do it. So clashes are inevitable; and their resolution demands a government having legal powers and the means of enforcing them. Regarding defence forces, most citizens will probably be unwilling to supply adequate financial support, especially when the danger, although real, is not starkly obvious.

The source of government authority. We have argued that civil society arises from human nature, in the sense that it is a requirement for a full human life. And we have just given reasons for the necessity of authority in society. So authority is a natural necessity. It is not from will, as though the citizens chose it even though they could reasonably have chosen to dispense with it.

But society has to exercise its authority through certain of its members, for a pure democracy (in the sense of government by everyone) is impracticable. Individuals, therefore, exercise authority; but they do so as representing the society, and their authority is from society.

The Purpose of Government Defined

In the light of what has been said, we can define the purpose of government as: **The promotion of the due social order in the whole civic community.**

Promotion. A thing can be promoted either negatively, by defending it from interference, or positively, by actions designed directly to cause the desired effect. It is primarily in the first way that governments should act. If they are in accord with the natural order they will be occupied mostly with seeing that the conditions of a free and healthy society are not tampered with. It is not a genuine function of government, for instance, to operate as a tourist office or as an organiser of sport. In general, the government must not do what other bodies, or individuals, can do.

Etymologically the word govern is from the Greek and Latin for the steering or navigating of a ship, and this indicates the rightful place of government. The navigator does not set the course; his job is to see that the ship remains on the course that has been set. Likewise, the task of the governing authorities of a country is to see that the course determined by the nature of human society is adhered to.

Due social order. This book is primarily about the economy, but governmental functions extend much further, embracing the whole of society. Since society is more than an arrangement for material advancement, and is for the development of the total person, the government's scope includes an interest in cultural, moral and spiritual values. So if human values are being attacked by pornographic magazines or videos, it comes within the scope of government authority to ban them.

The whole civic community. The natural purpose of government is the good of the community as such, not that of any individual or group within the community. This follows from the nature of government, which is an authority over the whole civic body, and is required so that the community may reach its full potential. The true end is perverted whenever the good of any part is chosen by the state instead of the good of the whole. This is a terrible abuse in existing societies. Politicians put themselves or their parties ahead of the nation's interests. Or unwarranted favours are bestowed on particular industries, cultural associations, and so on.

The Common Good of Political Society

In chapter two we analysed the crucially important concept of the common good, defining it: **A non-exclusive benefit, desired as a social end, and achieved through association**. Alternatively: **A good desired in common, achieved in common, and possessed in common**. These characteristics are found in the end or purpose of government.

Firstly, the common good of a group is the good to which it is ordered, and therefore is its unifying principle. It is *desired as a social end*. This is verified of the end under discussion: **The promotion of the due social order in the whole civic community**. This is the *raison d'être* of society as a political organism, and the desire for it provides the dynamism for its actualisation.

Secondly, the political common good is *achieved through association*; it is caused in common by the members of the political community in so far as they act as a community. For this reason we should not think of the political order too narrowly as something constituted by politicians - something belonging to "the government". We all have our part in contributing to the political common good. We do this by voting for those who will exercise the office of government; but we also contribute in whatever way we promote the harmony that should exist. And we damage that harmony by acting contrary to it - as in electing politicians who will further our interests by unjust discrimination against others, or by lobbying for advantages to which we are not entitled. Doing so, we share in that "most vicious injustice," as Colin Clark rightly names it, "...the practice whereby the state uses taxes to pay groups of citizens, not from motives of justice, not from motives of real charity, but for the purpose of securing support for the party at the next election."[5]

Thirdly, the political common good is such that it can be enjoyed by everyone without being diminished. It is *a non-exclusive benefit*. It is common in a distributive sense, not in a collective sense. It is not like a well from which all the people in the vicinity are allowed to drink, for the water is being appropriated and used up. The well is possessed collectively. But the common good generated by the political community does not diminish although enjoyed by millions. The social order of justice and harmony promoted by the politically organised community is an environment from which each person can benefit without reducing the good available for the rest, and which indeed tends to increase, to diffuse itself more perfectly.

Political society, with its laws and sanctions, is therefore a very great good. We are speaking, of course, of society in so far as it is rightly constituted. When, on the contrary, societies get away from that order, the resulting evils are great. The classical definition of evil is *privation of good*. Evil is the absence of a good that should be present. So its degree is measured by that good. If I lose a finger, this is not as bad as losing an arm, for it is the deprivation of a lesser good. Likewise, the greater the good that would flow from a healthy political system, the greater the evil when our existing political system departs from what it should be. Then, seeing the evils afflicting us, and seeing how the politicians and the legal system have contributed to them, we may be tempted to reject the body politic as such. But this would be to reject an excellent thing, a sublime thing, instead of rejecting its corruption. Hence Aristotle says: "He who first founded the state was the greatest of benefactors."[6]

References

[1] Murray Rothbard, *Power and Market*, Menlo Park, California, Institute for Humane Studies, 1970, pp. 134f., original italics.
[2] *Ibid.*, p. 2.
[3] *Ibid.*, p. 4.
[4] *Ibid.*, p. 5, original italics.
[5] Colin Clark, *Taxmanship*, London, Institute of Economic Affairs, 1964, p. 16.
[6] Aristotle, *Politics*, book I, chapter 2, 1253a, 30.

18

When the Government Leaves its Orbit

The Prevalence of Statism

Not content to remain in their own sphere, or not knowing what that sphere is, governments all over the world usurp the place, and therefore the rights, of others. This is statism, or **exorbitance of the government**: the government leaves its proper orbit. An alternative definition is: **Violation by the government of the principle of subsidiarity**.

A sign of statism is found in the huge amounts needed by modern governments. In the United States, from 1900 till the first World War, total government expenditure - federal, state and local - was never above 12 per cent of national income. During the second World War it reached about 50 per cent. In the early 1990s, total government expenditure was about 35 per cent of GDP.[1] Government figures for 1995 show 15.9 per cent of total federal spending going to programmes for the poor, including 4.3 per cent for international help, under the headings: medicaid, security, food and nutrition, housing assistance, social services, international development and aid.[2]

Not only are vast sums being spent, but the waste is colossal - through maladministration, cheating, benefits going to those who do not really need them. The Friedmans' comment on 1978 welfare programme figures is pertinent: "If these funds were all going to the 'poor', there would be no poor left - they would be among the comfortably well-off, at least."[3]

In recent years government health costs have expanded in the industrialised countries. Significantly, services cost far more when public funds are provided, which in turn leads governments to impose controls in an effort to keep costs to a reasonable level. But they still escalate, with the threat of further controls.

Education is another area where government spending and activity have vastly escalated. Yet complaints grow concerning deficiencies in state run education, and the educational establishment lobbies for even larger funds.

Let us try to get a more concrete picture of the ramifications of statism by looking at the three areas of education, medical care and social security. In each case we need to remember the principle of subsidiarity: if a thing can be done by a smaller group or by individuals, it should not be assigned to a higher group.

Education. It is usually taken for granted that governments have a right to establish and run schools. But if we apply the principle of subsidiarity we arrive, I contend, at the opposite conclusion: they are going beyond their orbit in doing so; it is an example of statism.

Firstly, the large number of private schools provide the evidence that an educational system does not have to be state run in order to function well. And if it is not necessary for something to be state run, it should not be. Secondly, the danger of indoctrination is worse when governments run a large part of the educational facilities, whether at primary, secondary or tertiary level. They can make it difficult for views they dislike to be expressed and, more insidiously, can inculcate a particular mindset, thus making it hard for students even to see a contrary point of view. Moreover, the views being inculcated may be those of pressure groups with an influence over the government, rather than any particularly favoured by the government itself. Granted this can happen in private schools too; but state schools are peculiarly vulnerable because of the pressure governments can exert, and because of the strength that comes from public funding - especially through restriction of the options open to parents when they are financially disadvantaged in choosing private schools.

If the state should not own schools or universities, to what extent should it be involved with them? What about supervision of the content and standards of teaching, and of providing funding?

Again, the principle is that the state should do only what is necessary. More is necessary at present than should be. If the great majority of the schools are owned and run by the state, with parents at a severe financial disadvantage when they want to move their children to a private school, this will encourage inefficiency, bringing a need for a degree of state scrutiny of the curricula and standards that would otherwise be unnecessary. But under private enterprise, competition among schools would see to it that they did what their employers, the parents, wanted. And parents, on the whole, know better than the government what is best for their children. Little government supervision would be required.

As for public funding, although its abolition now would cause hardship, it would be unnecessary in a normal economy. Following the reforms discussed in earlier chapters, people would ordinarily have the means of paying school fees. When they are paid by the taxpayers instead of by parents, there is no less expense (rather, there is considerably more, because of the reduced efficiency); they are only obtained from a larger section of the population. In extreme cases where genuine hardship existed, due to sickness or other causes, private benevolence, not public funds, would be the solution. Here again, what can be done privately should not be done by the state.

In the present situation, the widely discussed but little used voucher system is the best answer. With the parents given a government voucher to be presented to the school of their choice, and the school claiming from the government the amount specified, parents would have a degree of freedom in the choice of a school which they now generally lack.

Medical care. When hospitals are state owned, or doctors are government employees, this is another example of statism. What of hospital or medical expenses? Is the government justified in taxing people to pay the whole or part of those expenses? In so far as some are unable to pay for their own medical needs without severe hardship, a humane society (and it is *natural* for society to be humane) will provide help. But that does not mean the help should necessarily come from government funds. It should not unless there is no reasonable alternative. Under a natural economy the vast majority could pay for their own health care. Participant funded health insurance schemes would exist. Additionally, as with education, private benevolence would play a part. But government assistance would be unnecessary; and therefore its provision would violate the principle of subsidiarity.

Social security. There is a profusion of social security benefits: old age pensions, unemployment benefits, child endowment; as well as associated aids like housing assistance and food coupons. Here again is the spectre of pauper legislation. Government provision of benefits, without necessity, is another manifestation of statism. And the fact that it is necessary to provide them today on a massive scale shows our social order to be far removed from what it should be. In a naturally functioning economy, little unemployment would exist, and therefore no big payouts in unemployment benefits. Higher returns to workers would normally provide enough to pay for their children's upbringing without a subsidy from the community. They would also be able to save enough for their retirement.

Take housing. It is a major expense, but in a natural economy would be reduced immensely through the near elimination of land prices and the reduction of interest rates.

There may seem to be something unfair in the father of a large family having to support his wife and children as well as himself, while a single person, with no dependents, receives the same wage. But various elements must be taken into account. For one thing, the single person is left in a better position to save for marriage, and then be better able to support a family, rather than if taxed to provide child endowment funds. And in the case of those who do not marry, it is likely they will need larger savings in old age, whereas the parents of a family, especially a big family, should receive aid from them if necessary. The fact that, so often today in the industrialised nations, many parents cannot count on help from their children is due in part to the welfare state mentality which expects the government to do what the family should do.

A great deal of current social welfare expense stems from problems in the home, notably from the break-up of families. A crucial factor is the large proportion of mothers who are forced to work on economic grounds, often to keep up the payments on a crippling mortgage. Hence the phenomenon of latch-key children, deprived for long hours of the care of a mother. Hence, too, the strain so many women are under in struggling to do two jobs, one in the workplace and one in the home.

Some general points. The following points, already adverted to, deserve emphasis.

Firstly, under a natural system people could much better provide for their own needs; and it is also to be anticipated that private help, through charitable organisations and so on, would be greater than today if required, for the community would be much more prosperous, wealth would not be drained away in taxation, and the orientation towards private help would be stronger, rather than relying on the government. George Gilder states: "Before 1935 over half of all welfare came from private charity. Now the figure is less than 1 per cent."[4]

Secondly, when governments supply goods and services, or they are paid for from public funds, there is less efficiency than in private hands; so less would be spent privately for the same results. This comes out clearly in the Grace Commission Report, the result of an analysis of government spending in the United States, undertaken to show how waste can be reduced.

The Commission concluded that more than $424 billion could be cut from the federal deficit over a three-year period by eliminating waste and inefficiency.

Note a few instances cited in the Report. If debt collection methods were streamlined, an estimated $9.3 billion reduction in the federal deficit could be achieved in three years.[5] Improvements in the health-care system would save an estimated $28.9 billion in three years.[6] As an example of government costs compared with private enterprise costs, the Veterans Administration's construction expense for a nursing home bed was $61,250, compared to $15,900 for a leading private sector nursing home operator, Beverly Enterprises.[7] "By privatizing government programs in only eight areas, the Grace Commission asserts that savings and revenue enhancements totaling $28.4 billion can be realized."[8]

Thirdly, with greater freedom from government intervention, greater scope would exist to obtain what we desired. In education, for instance, a variety of schools, with different methods and emphases, would offer a degree of choice unavailable today, especially for people who are not wealthy.

Fourthly, with enlarged freedom, desirable qualities would more easily be fostered. The increased independence would bring an enhanced sense of responsibility - instead of the "Why doesn't the government do something" attitude so prevalent today. Individual initiative thrives when the liberty to exercise it exists, a truth vividly shown by contrasting the economic stagnation under Communism with the relative freedom enjoyed by the so-called capitalist countries. Communism has provided a stark example of what happens when people are deprived of liberty. How much greater would be the contrast if during the long decades of Communist oppression the allegedly free world had really been free!

The Psychology of Statism

The menace of statism is ever present in society, for it issues from tendencies in human nature, including greed, the desire for power and the desire for prestige. A good tendency, sometimes having the same unfortunate result, is a desire to help the needy.

The welfare state offers opportunities (apparently) to get things with less effort than we would otherwise have to expend. We have seen that effort-saving can be perversely achieved by imposing effort unfairly on others. If the government offers, say, $10,000 of public money to first-home buyers, the temptation will arise to accept it, without considering whether we should impose this burden on our fellow taxpayers. And similarly with all the personal advantages associated with the welfare state. Most of us, whether we admit it or not, can easily be bribed by politicians. Surely one of the most blatant features of the average election campaign is the assortment of privileges offered to various sections of the voters - at the expense of others. A party that refused to buy votes would stand little or no chance of election.

Greed plays a big part in the maintenance and advancement of statism. So does the drive for power or for prestige by business men, public servants, politicians. The dismantling of the apparatus of privileges would diminish their position, whereas its growth enhances it.

A genuine desire to help the needy ranks as an important factor. The real help given by the welfare state is seen, and is contrasted with the cold indifference and cruel exploitation found in society. Indifference and exploitation are only too often realities of our present private sector, and it is easy to conclude that the sole realistic alternative is government control.

What are not seen (because prevented from existing) are the initiatives stifled by government action. Particularly tragic is the frustration of the abilities of outstanding individuals, who in conditions of greater freedom would have used their genius to enrich society. The major discoveries come from an almost infinitesimal percentage of the human race, and every suppression of initiative carries the danger of aborting some precious discovery.

Objections

Proposals to restrict government activities are met with various objections, some of which have already been discussed. Fears are expressed that reductions in government controls will result in too much power being placed in private hands; or that the law of the jungle will prevail; or that the consumer will suffer.

Take privatisation. A proposal to privatise postal services or state banks will be met with the objection that the government would lose its power to control those concerns in the public interest.

A first point is that government control over the public sector is very limited - a fact which becomes clear when politicians try to reform things. Such is the weight of inertia and the force of selfish interests in the public service that reforms are often almost impossible. It is easier to control the private sector, for government authority is easier to enforce there on account of competition or potential competition. Firms that do not comply are in danger of being replaced by those that do. Further, when complaints are made about the public service, the tendency of the parliamentarians officially in charge is to deny the problem, for the criticism is seen as detracting from their competence. But if complaints are made about a private firm, a parliamentarian can improve his popularity with voters by rectifying the problem. In general, if the common good requires special government supervision (as in financial institutions), this will be easier when the organisations being supervised are in the private sector.

Some fear that a drastic restriction of government action will unleash a variety of effects stemming from the drive for power and profit on the part of private enterprise, especially big business. Safety standards will fall; scarce resources will be consumed in the pursuit of present profits to the detriment of future generations; the weak will be dominated by the strong; the consumer will lack protection.

A degree of government supervision, with intervention where necessary, will always be required. But intervention must be a last resort, and little would be needed if the principles examined in this work were followed.

We are currently witnessing a welcome retreat from the public sector. Madsen Pirie sees 1979 as the turning point in the movement to dismantle state industries, regulations and transfer payments. "Although the retreat from the public sector began in 1979 with a lead from Britain, it has since been taken up in more than 100 countries around the world. Most of these countries took lessons drawn from the British experience, and more than half of them sent teams to visit Britain to learn how privatization was achieved there."[9]

Caution is needed, though. John Vickers and George Yarrow observe that "Unless effective competition and/or regulation are introduced, the privatization of firms with market power brings about private ownership in precisely the circumstances where it has least to offer."[10] They consider the British government to have been sensible in focussing initially "on companies such as Amersham, British Aerospace, Cable and Wireless, Enterprise Oil, and Jaguar, all of which operate in reasonably competitive conditions."[11] But "British privatization policy for firms with monopoly power (e.g. British Telecom (BT) and British Gas) has been seriously flawed."[12]

Although the privatisation movement is encouraging, the economic structure is radically defective. Statism is inevitable if the natural economy does not operate, for government laws must then attempt tasks that would be unnecessary if natural laws were not suppressed.

References

1 Samuelson and Nordhaus, *Economics*, New York, McGraw-Hill, 1995, p. 278.
2 Office of Management and Budget, Budget of the United States Government, 1995.
3 M. and R. Friedman, *Free to Choose*, Melbourne, Macmillan, 1980, p. 92.
4 George Gilder, *Wealth and Poverty*, New York, Basic Books, 1981, p. 112.
5 W.R. Kennedy and R.W. Lee, *A Taxpayer Survey of the Grace Commission Report*, Ottawa, Illinois, Green Hill Publishers, 1984, p. 34.
6 *Ibid.*, p. 53.
7 *Ibid.*, p. 81.
8 *Ibid*, p. 90.
9 M. Pirie, *Privatization*, Aldershot, Wildwood House, 1988, p. 295.
10 Vickers and Yarrow, *Privatization: An Economic Analysis*, Cambridge, Massachusetts, The MIT Press, 1988, p. 427.
11 *Ibid.*, p. 426.
12 *Ibid.*, p. 427.

19

Current Economic Problems

Since evil is the lack of a good that should be present, economic evils are a lack of the economic goods of abundance, leisure and the saving of effort. And as the common good is fostered especially by equality of opportunity, its absence is due especially to inequality of opportunity. But inequality of opportunity is due mainly to privilege.

Those conclusions follow from the investigation we have pursued, and we can illustrate them by reviewing some specific economic problems.

The public debt. A large public debt plagues many countries. It burdens taxpayers in the same way as individuals in debt are burdened by the constant paying of interest. Certainly to the extent that the borrowed sum is put to productive use it helps pay for itself, like any productive investment; but much government borrowing is a non-productive expense. The situation is aggravated by a fall in the value of the national currency, for this means that more currency, since it is no longer worth so much, has to be paid in interest to foreign lenders. The government, therefore, tries to keep up the price of the currency, which involves interfering with international trade by stimulating exports while discouraging imports.

Just as extravagant individuals borrow to maintain their extravagance, governments that go beyond their proper sphere resort to borrowing to help pay for their exorbitance. It is more popular than taxes! But the exorbitance entails privilege, both because the state acts in a privileged way by usurping the functions of its citizens, and because of the handouts to favoured groups.

Over-powerful firms. There are fears that big firms, notably vast international corporations, pose a grave threat to stability and economic freedom. But where do they get their power? Largely from governments. Think of the state subsidies to the motor industry, and the favouritism of import regulations that hamper competition. Big companies can exert great pressure on governments, often with the help of trade unions whose members' jobs may be at risk; and the privileges they extract allow them to dominate the market still further. William Simon writes of his experience as US Secretary of the Treasury in the 1970s: "I watched with incredulity as businessmen ran to the government in every crisis, whining for handouts or protection from the very competition that has made this system so productive..."[1]

Again privilege is at the root of the problem. If the government ceased to grant favours, and acted to protect rights violated by anti-competitive behaviour, there would be no need to worry about the menace of giant firms.

Taxation. The complexity of taxation laws continues to grow, together with the labour needed to keep up with them, the labour of collecting taxes and pursuing tax evaders, even the labour of preparing returns. Argument persists, too, about the merits of different taxes, about the alleged unfairness of some compared with others, about their distorting effects. It is a subject where consensus seems impossible; and the reason surely is that taxation is unnatural.

When tax takes over forty per cent of national income, as often happens today, the burden is crushing. Tax evasion becomes almost an industry, and citizens who are usually honest and truthful turn to concealment and untruthful statements in their returns. Unfairness abounds, for not all are equally able to evade taxes.

Admittedly, governments currently need this revenue. But why? Because of privilege. The basic privilege is that accorded to land owners in permitting them to appropriate the revenue which, from its nature, belongs to the community. Then there are the privileged groups, and they are legion, supported by public funds. Nor must we forget the privileges assigned by the government to itself in usurping the functions of others. These usurped functions - in medical services, education and elsewhere - are usually paid for largely from public funds. A further factor is that a distorted economy, indeed a distorted social system, requires more funds than a healthy one - as when a large pool of unemployed need government help.

Inflation. The serious economic malady of inflation was discussed in chapter sixteen. We examined currency dilution, the action of powerful groups, rising land prices - all causes of inflation. But privilege lies at their root. The state misuses its authority to increase the money supply unduly; it encourages and condones the growth of pressure groups; it allows its proper revenue to remain in private hands, thus leading to escalating land prices.

High interest rates. Anyone struggling to pay off a home mortgage knows by experience the heavy burden of interest rates, as does any business person who is heavily in debt. Why are interest rates high? The question was examined in chapter nine, and has reference to points we have made above. Inflation is a strong factor, for investors want a return that will compensate for this. Taxation is important for the same reason. Excessive borrowing is a third influence, for it causes a greater demand for funds and therefore pushes up the price the lender can ask. Excessive borrowing occurs largely through faults in the economic and social system. It includes the government borrowing criticised above under the heading *The public debt*. It also includes borrowing motivated by tax advantages. Inflation, too, encourages people to borrow, with the idea of: "Get it now, before the price goes up." Borrowing for land is of major significance, absorbing colossal amounts.

John Maynard Keynes advocated "an increase in the volume of capital until it ceases to be scarce, so that the functionless investor will no longer receive a bonus..."[2] To the extent that excessive borrowing is eradicated, interest rates will weaken, for funds will be less scarce.

Here again we find privilege as a major cause of the problem, for privilege is bound up with inflation, taxation and borrowing.

Land prices. The buying price of land is of singular importance. High prices tend to bar people from owning land and therefore to put them at the mercy of owners. It is most obvious in poor countries, with tenant farmers, unable to afford to buy property, being forced to accept unjust conditions imposed on them by landlords. But it is a problem in any society, with people unable to afford a home because of the cost of land, or businesses in danger of bankruptcy in hard times when payments to the landlord cannot be met. Further, the cost of buying land leaves the buyer with that much less for other purposes. And if money has to be borrowed there is the added expense of interest payments - often totalling more than the land price. Assuming a loan of $50,000 and 262 monthly payments of $650, with an interest rate of 15 per cent, the total interest will be $120,479.

If the state took all but a small part of the return from sites, land prices would fall to a low level and the problems from this source would evaporate. Land would be easily affordable, and the crippling burden of repayments would be unknown. A powerful means of dominating the less fortunate would be relegated to the history books.

A healthy diversion of funds from land to industrial capital would occur, as the experience of Taiwan illustrates. Extensive land reforms were initiated in the 1950s. First the 37.5 per cent Land Reduction programme "set an upper limit for a tenant's farm rental at 37.5% of the total annual yield of the main crop and prohibited any extra payment charged by the landlord."[3] This was followed by the selling of government-owned land to the farmers, and the purchasing of land from landlords which was resold to the tenants.[4] In 1967 the President of the Chinese National Association of Industry and Commerce, C.F. Koo, stated that before the reforms landlords were usually unwilling to invest in industry. But through the reforms, "Capital which used to be active in land transactions or frozen in land has been given over to growing industry since the land reform and thus increased the rate of industrial employment."[5]

Once again privilege is the culprit - the privilege accorded site owners of retaining what belongs to society.

Recessions. A major problem plaguing the economy - trade cycles - is a persistent cause of unemployment when the cycle swings into its recession phase. Many factors contribute, mostly bound up with privilege in various forms. Government intervention, perhaps as a desperate attempt to correct maladies stemming from basic faults in the economy, often produces unemployment, as when demand is dampened down to combat inflation. There is also the effect of wage rigidities and of impediments to changing one's occupation; there are inflation, high interest rates, high taxes. But the effect of land speculation deserves special attention, particularly as its influence is generally underestimated.

A major way in which speculation leads to a recession is through its impact on home building. In Britain in 1976 the National Economic Development Office observed that the figures for Britain since 1959 show that "private sector home-building is one of the least stable components of GDP and makes a substantial and, recently, growing contribution to the overall cycle. In general, the private housebuilding cycle is in very close conformity with the overall cycle."[6] The influence is predominantly through the price of land, not the house. As the boom develops, land speculation intensifies, pushing up prices. This makes it ever harder for people to build, which results in a diminishing of construction activity; and this in turn, because of its crucial part in the economy, is a main cause of the ensuing slump.

Viewing land speculation as a whole, including industrial and commercial sites, we find speculation increasing as the boom gathers momentum, with speculators borrowing to buy land. In the later stages, greed and the gambling instinct prompt further recklessness. When it is eventually seen that land has become overpriced, prices drop. Then come the financial crashes and bankruptcies. The repercussions spread through the economy, sending it into recession.

Fred Harrison, documenting the American collapse of 1974, shows how, as yields came down on land overpriced by speculators, it was impossible for many to service their mortgages. The value of land trusts crashed, speculators and builders were forced into bankruptcy. "The Chase Manhattan Mortgage and Realty Trust, the country's largest, clung on until May Day, 1978, before it defaulted on more than $38m. in loan notes."[7]

The prominence of rising land prices in bringing about a recession is due to the difference between land and wealth (products) in relation to supply. With an increased demand for wealth, a demand that will temporarily raise prices, more wealth is produced to satisfy the demand; and the greater volume of production tends to reduce prices. But the quantity of land is fixed. Therefore a greater demand leads to a higher price. So as the economy expands, land prices rise, speculation intensifies, land becomes unaffordable, the building industry slows down and speculators are unable to service their loans.

Privilege looms large as a cause of recessions. It operates in all the factors enumerated. It is at the root of land prices, which could not possibly be more than minimal if the community received its proper revenue, instead of land owners appropriating it through the privilege currently allowed them.

Unemployment. The heartbreaking tragedy of involuntary unemployment can be traced to various sources, including excessive wages, obstacles to changing jobs and economic recessions.

Minimum wage laws always result in some people being excluded from employment, for ability, training and other considerations vary so much from person to person that there are always those whom it would be uneconomical to employ at the mandated wage. The number of employers willing to carry them will be too small to absorb them all. It was argued in chapter four that when competition is not operating effectively, minimum wage legislation may be the lesser of two evils. Still, a degree of unemployment will result. It is worse, obviously, if award wages are unrealistically high.

Obstacles to changing one's occupation lead to unemployment. Demand for workers in a particular occupation is constantly changing, so it is essential, if both an excess and a scarcity of applicants are to be minimised, that the greatest practicable flexibility in changing jobs be promoted.

Mass unemployment due to economic recessions is a recurring problem, and we have outlined some causes of recessions.

From an overall view of involuntary unemployment, the presence of privilege is clear. If freedom were not restricted by privilege, as discussed especially in chapter three, minimum wage laws would be superfluous. And without entry quotas and other barriers, job flexibility would be far greater. As for recessions, we have noted the major part played by privilege in various forms.

Poverty. A well-functioning economy creates an abundance of goods and services, which is the direct opposite of poverty. Therefore if the system leaves a big section of the population in a state of poverty, it must be radically defective.

The capital goods which so marvellously aid production may be lacking. Or the technology may be inappropriate for the situation. This can happen through the importation of advanced technology into countries not having the infrastructure and technical education to use it efficiently. When technology is concentrated in large cities, an imbalance is likely in the spread of population, with people moving to the cities in search of work - partly because the new technology, driving out less efficient older methods, has rendered them unemployed. But many who come to the cities lack the education or skills to use the new methods. As E.F. Schumacher demonstrates, the need in these conditions is for intermediate technology: above the primitive level it replaces, yet well below the high ratio of capital to labour of industrialised nations.

"At such a level of capitalisation, very large numbers of workplaces would be 'within reach' for the more enterprising minority within the district, not only in financial terms but also in terms of their education, aptitude, organising skill, and so forth."[8]

Writing of Latin America, Michael Novak claims that the key to the future lies "in one place only: the most rapid possible growth in the small business sector." Its facilitation will be "as fundamental to economic development in Latin America as it has been in other economically successful nations."[9]

If a society is riddled with injustice, if class structures oppress the poor, if education and opportunities are lacking, if technology is primitive or inappropriate, poverty will be widespread.

Even in a relatively prosperous country there may still be much poverty, and two main causes are unemployment (which we have looked at) and low wages. The freedom and competition examined in chapter three are a remedy for low wages, because they give workers the opportunities needed to better their position. Aggravating a low wage situation is the high cost of accommodation afflicting so many. And this, as shown earlier, is principally through high land prices.

Again we discover privilege to be the main underlying problem. Subtract privilege, with all its ramifications, and little poverty would remain.

Of course poverty comes in part from non-economic causes, such as excessive drinking or gambling, or from family break-ups. Writing of the United States, Frank F. Furstenberg Jn. and Andrew J. Cherlin report: "In 1988, among female-headed families, with children under 18, 45 per cent were poor. In contrast, 7 per cent of families headed by a married couple were living in poverty."[10]

However, even in these instances economic problems often play a big part. Conversely, social difficulties, with the ravaging effects they can have on the personality, make it harder to cope in the economy. Poverty tends to become self-perpetuating.

In Conclusion

We have outlined the basic principles of a natural order in economic life. It is an order that should exist, but which we must bring into being. Even today, when hampered and violated, it operates to some degree, and brings much prosperity. Our task is to understand it more clearly and work for its full actualisation.

Without it no economy can function well; none can avoid the maladies so evident throughout the world. If it could ever be fully implemented, it would not solve all human problems; but it would solve all serious economic problems. Its substantial implementation is certainly achievable, and will bring an economic golden age.

References

1. W.E. Simon, *A Time for Truth*, New York, Berkley Books, 1979, p. 210.
2. J.M. Keynes, *The General Theory of Employment, Interest and Money*, Cambridge, Macmillan, 1983 reprint, p. 376.
3. K.T. Li, *Economic Transformation of Taiwan*, London, Shepheard-Walwyn, 1988, p. 83.
4. *Ibid.*
5. C.F. Koo, "Land Reform and its Impact on Industrial Development in Taiwan," in *Land Reform in Developing Countries*, edited by Brown and Lin, University of Hartford, 1968, p. 374.
6. *Cyclical Fluctuations in the UK Economy, Discussion Paper 3*, London, NEDO, 1976, p. 15.

[7] Fred Harrison, *The Power in the Land*, London, Shepheard-Walwyn, 1983, p. 116.

[8] E.F. Schumacher, *Small is Beautiful*, London, Sphere Books, 1974, p. 150.

[9] Michael Novak, *This Hemisphere of Liberty*, Washington DC, American Enterprise Institute for Public Policy Research, 1990, p. 58.

Glossary

Association:	The union of many people to a common end.
Capital (true):	Wealth employed as an instrument of production.
(spurious):	Capitalisation of an unearned income.
Common good:	A non-exclusive benefit, desired as a social end, and achieved through association. **Alternative definition**: A good desired in common, achieved in common, and possessed in common. **The principal economic common good**: Abundance of goods and services. **Other economic common goods**: (a) Leisure. (b) Saving of effort. **Political common good**: Promotion of the due social order in the whole civic community.
Competition: (true):	Economic agents, all with a diversity of opportunities open to them, striving through exchange to provide or obtain labour, wealth or services.
(Spurious):	Economic agents, lacking diversity of opportunities, striving against each other to provide or obtain labour, wealth or services.

Credit:	Purchasing power obtained by means of a promise to pay.
Economics:	The science of wealth and services, as priced.
Evil:	Privation of good.
Inflation:	A fall in the value of money.
Interest (return on capital):	Recompense for the investment of capital.
Labour:	Exercise of human activity in production.
Land:	Natural resources, excluding human activity.
(More widely):	The natural environment, excluding human activity.
Leisure:	Freedom from economic activity.
Market:	The milieu of the social exchange of labour, wealth, services and money.
Money:	Generally acceptable medium of exchange which finalises a transaction. *(Spurious)*: A terminus of exchange masquerading as a medium.
Ownership:	The right to possess, use and dispose of a thing.
Price:	The measurement of relative command over human exertion.
(Alternative definition):	The quantification of value.
Privilege:	A power accorded by the state to some, with undue discrimination against others.
Production:	The process of satisfying human desire through the provision of wealth and services.

Property:	Things over which is had the right of possession, use and disposal. *private*: Property owned by one or more individuals, not by a society. *public*: Property owned by a society.
Return on capital :	see *Interest*.
Rent:	see *Site revenue*.
Saving of effort (principle of):	People seek to satisfy their wants with the least effort. (Economic principle of): In the economy all participants naturally tend to save effort through exchange.
Science:	Certain knowledge through an understanding of causes.
Service:	The satisfaction of desire by human exertion, without the production of wealth.
(Alternative definition):	Modification of the person, through human exertion, towards the satisfaction of desire.
Site revenue:	Return from situational advantages. In production: Return produced by - i.e., efficiently caused by - differential situational advantages. Outside production: Return induced by - ie, finally caused by - differential situational advantages. *Monopolistic*: Return irrespective of differential advantages. *Speculative*: Measure of the return expected from future situational advantages.
Statism:	Exorbitance of the government.
(Alternative definition):	Violation by the government of the principle of subsidiarity.
Subsidiarity (principle of):	What can be done by an individual or smaller group should not be assigned to a larger group.

Taxation: The taking of private property for public purposes.

Value: Command over human exertion.
from production: Command over human exertion, competitively determined, and arising from the expenditure of labour and capital.
without production: Command over human exertion, arising from unearned advantages.

Wages: Recompense for effort expended in production.

Wealth: Natural resources that have been modified by human exertion to make them fit, or more fit, for the satisfaction of desire.

Index

Y

Z